Ron Ridenour

CUBA: BEYOND THE CROSSROADS

Socialist Resistance, London

Socialist Resistance would be glad to have readers'
opinions of this book, its design and translations,
and any suggestions you may have for future
publications or wider distribution.

Socialist Resistance books are available at special
quantity discounts to educational and
non-profit organizations, and to bookstores.

To contact us, please write to:
Socialist Resistance,
PO Box 1109, London, N4 2UU, Britain
or email us at: contact@socialistresistance.net
or visit our website at: www.socialistresistance.net

Set in 11pt Joanna
Designed by Ed Fredenburgh
Published by Socialist Resistance
(second edition, revised April 2007)
Printed in Britain by Lightning Source
ISBN 0-902869-95-0
EAN 9 780902 869950

© Ron Ridenour, 2007
Readers are encouraged to visit
www.ronridenour.com
To contact the author,
please email ronr@mail.dk

Contents

	Acknowledgements	vi
	Introduction	vii
	Preface	viii
1	Return to Cuba	1
2	Comparing Living Standards	5
3	Tenacious Survival	12
4	The Blockade Squeeze	17
5	Enemies of the State	21
6	The Battle for Food	26
7	Life on the Farm	31
8	Feeding a Nation	35
9	From Farm to Table	39
10	On the Market	44
11	A Farewell to Farms	48
12	Health for All	51
13	Education for All	55
14	Exporting Human Capital	60
15	Media Openings	65
16	Cultural Rectification	69
17	Revolutionary Morality	73
18	The Big Challenge; forging communist consciousness	78
19	Fidel Leadership	82
20	Me and Fidel	89
21	Leadership after Fidel	93
22	Beyond the Crossroads	102
	CUBA: TENAZ PALMA REAL	108
	CUBA: TENACIOUS ROYAL PALM	109

Acknowledgements

I wish to thank "Morning Star" features editor Richard Bagley for his excellent editing of my 2006 series on Cuba today.
I am grateful to Walter Lippmann (www.walterlippmann.com) for his useage of the series in CubaNews@yahoogroups.com.
Duncan Chapple of Socialist Resistance has done a good job in completing the book.
In Cuba, I have had ample cooperation with Havana University's Cuban Economic Studies Center, especially drs. Omar Everleny Pérez Villanueva and Santiago Rodríguez Castellón.
I especially thank Guillermina Montero and Edgardo Rochet Blanco, both members of the José Fernandez UBPC farm cooperative, for their hospitality, insights and friendship.
Finally, I thank my friend Captain Antonio García Urquiolla, a former double agent for Cuba's security forces, who provided me with moral support.

"Mr Imperialists, we have absolutely no fear!"

Introduction

As a long-term writer about matters Cuban, Ron Ridenour's sometimes overused penchant for snide comments about Cubans and their government has, from time to time, irritated me, but his reporting is exemplary in its thoroughness and attention to detail.

His intimate insight into the day-to-day life of Cuban citizens and of the strenuous steps taken by the government to make sure that every Cuban has a basically sound quality of life, suggests that he has lived and worked in Cuba for ages, at various ground-level jobs, and is highly supportive of the social policies prevailing there.

Ron is not a political theoretician, but his devotion to revolutionary Cuba cannot be doubted. Some of his comments are deeply resonant of comments that you frequently hear Cubans coming out with on building sites. They bespeak a guarded tendency to belittle high ideals with mordantly humorous asides about low-level corruption. They remind me a bit of comments that I heard nuns working on literacy projects in El Salvador in the 1970s make among themselves—a sort of "Let's not sound so holy".

In Ron's case, it gives his writing the salty bite of authenticity in a Damon Runyan sort of way, but it is obvious that he regards the Cuban Revolution as a pearl of great price. It seems to me that his sort of provocative and knowledgeable writing, if widely enough circulated, could do much to counter the routinely uninformed knee-jerk hostile coverage usually accorded Cuba by the media.

As for me, I see that pearl as leading the way in showing us how to transcend the mess we are in and I thank Ron for his literary style.

Theodore MacDonald wrote these words as part of two letters-to-the-editor published in the "Morning Star" (May 23 and August 29, 2006). MacDonald is a prolific lecturer and author of several books, including on Cuba's health-education and social developments. He has held university chairs in Education, Health and Mathematics, and has taught at several universities in many lands. He lives in Littlehampton with his wife Chris.

Preface

"Cuba's revolution—its ideology and economy, the society as a whole—is in crisis. Contemporary reality is changing rapidly in confusing directions." I wrote this when introducing "Cuba at the Crossroads", an anthology of articles written mainly for the English daily "Morning Star", in 1994.

Cuba for me is the home of my heart. I align myself with the Cuban revolution, with its warts and its valiant efforts to humanize people and be independent.

Born in the "devil's own country" of a WASP military family, I experienced the pains and indignities of US imperial domination, its racism at home and abroad, its chauvinism and jingoism. I learned the true character of the "American Dream" especially as an airman in its air force in the late 1950s. In shame of and anger for what the US really does against peoples, I took responsibility and joined the budding student and anti-war movements, and supported the black, brown and Native American liberation movements.

My first demonstration was in Los Angeles, California against the April 1961 Bay of Pigs invasion. The Cuban revolution inspired me. Throughout the 1960s-70s, I was primarily an activist and participatory journalist.

In 1980, I moved to Denmark and married Grethe Porsgaard. I lived for several months in Sandinista Nicaragua in 1982 and 1984.

In 1987, the Ministry of Culture invited me to work for Editorial José Martí publishing house as an editorial consultant for its English department. I lived on a normal Cuban peso wage with ration card between 1988 and the spring of 1996. In 1991, Editorial José Martí published my first book concerning Cuba, "Backfire: The CIA's Biggest Burn". It is about double agents, 26 Cubans and one Italian, who had ostensibly accepted the CIA's offer to be their agents. In reality, they informed the Cuban Ministry of Interior security department, DSE, about this enemy offer and then worked for Cuba as double agents.

In the autumn of 1992, I left the publishing house and sailed on a Cuban container ship, Giorita, to Europe where I conducted a solidarity tour. I returned to Cuba in the spring of 1993, sailing on another Cuban container ship, Rose Islands. I was then "Morning Star's" correspondent until 1996. My regular job, though, was as a translator and features writer for the Cuban news agency, Prensa Latina, until my brother died in the spring of 1996. After attending his funeral, I returned to Denmark to be close to my family and write more about Cuba.

Like "Cuba at the Crossroads", my 1997 book "Cuba: a `Yankee reports", which the Germany's Papyrossa published as "Kuba: ein `Yankee berichtet", also deals with how Cuba was coping following the fall of its political and trading partners in Eastern Europe and the Soviet Union.

I followed Cuba for a decade from Denmark and returned to Cuba during the first three months of 2006, in order to compare the state of affairs with the first half of the 1990s. This book is a revision, update and amplification of 22 articles, which appeared in "Morning Star" from April 20 to August 1, 2006. I have also revised the English style to that of American English.

This book deals with Cuba's progress and challenges, the continued and stepped-up United States aggression and Cuba's responses, the battle to forge a healthy economy and an ideology which can unify people. I worked on a cooperative farm, reporting on agricultural advances and distribution of food. I also look into social developments: the universal health care system and the miraculous cure for many types of blindness, known as Operation Miracle, the educational system, humanitarian foreign mission, and some of Cuba's contradictions and challenges.

Like tens of millions of other fighters for justice, and even by-standers just in the way, I have received personal punishment at the repressors' bloody hands. I've been jailed a dozen times, tortured in a Mississippi jail cell and a Costa Rican prison. My father "divorced" me 27 years before his death, taking his ostracism to his grave. The mother of my two children stole them from me "legally", and I have not seen them in 26 years. The FBI got me black-listed from the mass media. The CIA and Los Angeles Police Red Squad spread black propaganda that I was one of theirs, which few radicals bought yet it had its sour affect.

That is a picture of what we can expect to happen when we struggle against the evil profiteering system. Yet when we win battles, and eventually the war—as Cubans have—we reclaim the streets and interweave in growing harmony and love. That dream, and possible reality, is worth all the struggle and incriminations.

Long live the Revolution!

Chapter One:
Return to Cuba

Right from the start, I was impressed by the advances.

The aircraft landed at Havana's new airport, terminal three—a modern complex, attractively decorated and clean. Customs and service workers performed quicker and more efficiently in serving travelers than when I lived in Cuba. Furthermore, it soon became clear that service workers were generally more attentive and efficient. This was so not only where sales are in the newly created convertible currency, known as *cucs*, valued at 1 to $1.10, but also in peso places.

(Cuba had recently abolished the use of US dollars. Those possessing dollars must convert them to the new convertible currency in Cuban banks.)

After a night in one of Havana's *casa particular* (private homes whose owners are supposed to pay a tax to rent a room or two), I looked up an old friend. Bill, the former "outlaw" Black Panther loaned me his bicycle.

I found an apartment for rent to Vedado, a central Havana district, and began to tour the city and province. I noticed few bicycles and many more automobiles, scooters and motorcycles.

Havanans viewed this as progress because not many care to cycle, according to experienced cyclists. In the first part of the Special Period—the government's term for survival reforms being enacted since the fall of European state socialism—there were hundreds of thousands cycling Havanans.

Cuba imported over one million bikes from China and started making its own. But the factory was now closed. Cyclists say the bikes were poorly made and there were never enough spare parts and tires. The only new bikes being sold were European imports and are sold only in cucs. Yet in the countryside and in most provinces, there were more bicycles and most were the old Chinese or Cuban makes.

My old friend Rogelio, who worked in the foreign ministry, greeted me with: "Good to see you back in the home of your heart."

When I asked about a mutual friend, a state security officer, Rogelio said, "I haven't seen him in years. With all the changes going on, I don't know what he is doing. He could be selling croquettes on the street for all I know."

In the coming days, I learned that former acquaintances, well educated with good positions—ship officers, journalists and editors in the publishing world, middle-level institution leaders—had left their respectable jobs with low pay to become self-employed in gastronomy, as taxi chauffeurs, office clerks in foreign joint venture firms and in tourism. This tendency had begun in the mid-1990s but had become more generalized.

In contrast to a plethora of prostitutes and hustlers, however, these opportunists had become rare. I never frequent tourist spots where some prostitutes are said to be, but there were fewer and they were not walking the streets.

Some Cubans joined the brain drain, abandoning Cuba not for ideological reasons but for better economic opportunities. The captain of Seaweed, a tanker I had sailed with in the 1990s, had stayed in Ecuador after taking cargo there. Another friend, a philosophy professor, moved to Canada. Quite a number of athletes, musicians, technicians, even a journalist colleague had abandoned Cuba for its enemy, the warrior country of my birth.

My first boss, the director of Editorial José Mart, had been a thoroughly uncritical Fidelista. He was fired some years ago for incompetence. He remained in Cuba but had taken up writing for a Spanish Catholic magazine, which supports "anti-Castroism".

Others, like Maya, a professor of English teachers, got promoted to her job of choice with opportunities to travel abroad. She had taught Mexican natives and had earned hard currency with which to buy appliances for her cozy apartment. She had benefited from free higher education like hundreds of thousands of other professionals who volunteer for foreign missions. While "resolving daily problems", they also concretely help people where they are sent.

Some view this cynically, others as practical. Most agree that Cubans and Cuba are seen by more and more millions of suffering people in the "third world" as the "Big One" when it comes to humanitarian solidarity. Operation Miracle is a good example.

I first heard of this recent Cuban invention, a cure for many blindnesses—cataracts, retractile disorders, corneal leucoma, myopias and strabismus, and, later, glaucoma—from a criminologist friend. Fernando had retired from the ministry of interior (pensioned at 300 pesos) and opened a *paladar*, a private restaurant legal only in one's home and limited to 12 customers at a time. Owners must not hire employees but these rules were not systematically enforced.

Fernando complained that he was viewed as one of the "new rich", and that the state gastronomic world did not enjoy the competition. So many *paladars* were closed. In Fernando's district, the preferred Playa, only 17 then remained, compared with 187 a decade ago.

Fernando struggled to find a bright side in his contradictory mindset. "Look into Operation Miracle. There's a positive story."

By December 2005, the simple and quick Cuban-devised operation had cured 210,000 persons in 25 countries within 18 months usage. Most of them, 150,000, were Venezuelans, but 36,000 were Cubans.

Cubans no longer suffer blindness and other illnesses caused by poor nutrition, as they did in the mid-1990s, when a neuritis epidemic caused sensory disturbances in over 50,000 persons. At this time, Cubans consumed a daily average of 3300 calories and 82 grams protein. In 1993, the average consumption was 1863 calories and 46 grams protein. WHO recommends 2400 calories and 72 grams of protein.

But not all Cubans were so pleased with the fantastic success their medical science had achieved in foreign missions. Even my former editor and staunch Communist party leader, Maritza, was upset about one of these developments.

Because she had been a leading journalist, Maritza had access to the Ministry of Health. She had felt forced to speak personally to the minister, in order to assure an eye operation for her husband. He had suffered partial blindness for two to three years during which he awaited an operation. After the minister ordered an operation, he could see once again.

Many felt that many institutions, including health care staff, were lethargic, indifferent and practiced personal favoritism. Some complain about this and the lack of adequate housing when pointing to the top floors of Cuba's tallest apartment building, Focsa, where I used to live. Several floors were being filled with Venezuelans brought in for the Operation Miracle cure.

The complainers seem to say, "You can't eat morality." At the same time, Maritza slammed the door on my face when I suggested that the majority, at least Havanans, lacked revolutionary morality.

Sigi had been Seaweed's first mate when I sailed with her. He earned a captain's certificate but never received his own ship. There were more qualified people than positions. Sigi is a mixture of European and African bloods, and proudly claims to have native Taino roots. Sigi had earlier applied for a pension but the monthly 264 pesos didn't reach. At 69, he was still sailing and earned twice that in pesos plus two dollars in convertible currency each day he sails.

Sigi gave me his view of Cuban traits:

"We are a people in love with pleasure: sports, entertainment, drinking, relaxing, sex. Men are womanizers; women are flirtatious. We are an amiable, joyful people, always in love or soon to be, and caring affectionately for those in our lives."

Cuba was still changing rapidly but not in such confusing directions as when I left, and Cubans clearly live better materially. As the saying goes: "We are born poor" (few resources) "and die rich" (of rich country diseases).

One of the problems, however, is that most I spoke with do not feel they live well enough. They don't care to compare themselves with the poor in the world. They complain of shortcomings, are even busier finding solutions to their daily problems, and focus more on themselves. As one friend reflected, "We are obstinate and spoiled."

The post-Soviet reforming process had resulted in greater concentration on individually assigned work tasks. Most work centers were now required to financially balance their own budgets. The government still basically controlled society but had decentralized some authority. It owned and operated less of the economy than it once had—about three-fourths production, services and employees. The remainder was run by joint-venture companies plus the growing numbers of self-employed.

With more self-reliance came greater production but, perhaps, less "caring affectionately for those in our lives".

Chapter Two:
Comparing Living Standards

An entire top floor of Juan Carlos and Lily's large house was mine for the duration at 550 *cucs* a month (605 US dollars equivalent). The spacious flat (100m2) was more than I needed: three large rooms, a bathroom with functioning flush toilet, adequate kitchen, and two terraces.

That rental—which was reasonably priced for a private rental (*casa particular*) in Vedado district—took 60% of my monthly income. Cubans have more of their income to spend than I did since no one can pay more than 10% of their wage for rent. A decade ago, 70% of Cubans owned their own flats. In 2006, 85% owned their homes. Cubans automatically own their residences once the state has been paid the original and actual construction costs.

My hosts were middle-aged professionals. Juan Carlos had been in the state's tourist business until his heart weakened. He then took on renting rooms to foreign visitors. He saw to paying the state a room-rental tax (325 *cucs* a month), and that the housemaid performed her tasks and was paid.

His wife, Lily, was a librarian at the José Martí center. Their son Carlos Alberto was in third grade and spent much of his free time in his own room listening to music and singing into a microphone. Lily's brother, Ernesto, his wife Barbara—both well-paid engineers—and their daughter lived in a smaller house in the back of the property. Lily's near-deaf aunt owned the house. She was a founder of the revolutionary woman's organization FMC.

The state had all but stopped its maintenance-service function of repairing appliances and residences—except for damage caused by natural catastrophes. Since this family was fortunate to have space to rent to foreigners in convertible currency, they could afford a carpenter and repairmen when necessary.

Benito, the carpenter, told me he had retired a decade ago as "a work director" and "began working." Benito was a founder of the new Communist party (1965), the armed forces and the ministry of interior. Making ends meet by finding ways to acquire convertible currency in addition to one's peso wage or pension had become common practice.

"My family" invited me to Christmas-eve dinner, and to watch end-of-year state parliamentary. I brought plenty of my name. Ron means rum in Spanish. Cubans have a warm and imaginative sense of humor. Eight-year old Carlos Alberto created a ditty about my name: "My name is Ron. I walk the streets--waiting for someone to drink me."

Advances

Some of the year's advances, reported by the parliament, cropped up in heated conversations we had in the house. Nobody wanted to admit that they were living better than a few years before; in fact, better now, in many respects, than when dependent upon the Soviet Union.

Barbara, for example, complained incessantly that she had "sweat blood" for two years to acquire the necessary convertible currency to buy a washing machine, and five years before that to buy a Phillips television set. The fact that this was *possible* did not penetrate as a positive, nor did my comparison with the vast majority of people in the world who do not have this possibility.

I am normally quite critical of government postulations, even the rare government which seeks to serve the broad public, such as Cuba's, but I often found myself defending the government and its necessarily-evil economic reforms to many Cubans.

The year of three hurricanes and a long drought had cost Cuba $3.65 billion in damage to crops, residences, schools, heath care centers and infrastructure. But no one had died in most of these hurricanes, because the people-oriented government evacuates everyone in time. Nor did anyone go hungry. And, despite the heavy losses, the 2005 economic growth rate was the *greatest* in its revolutionary history: 11.8%.

Tourism grew 12.3% with 2.3 million visitors at a profit of 32% investments-expenses.

Industry total increase was 4.6%. The greatest profit came from the 30,000-ton nickel production.

Transportation for the public grew enormously—Passenger train trips by 7.7%; cargo by 13.3%. Cuba bought 12 modern locomotives from China. National workers repaired 57 locomotives and 1733 wagons. Intra-provincial bus transportation increased by 49% with the importation of 200 modern Yutong Chinese buses. Cuba was importing thousands of buses and trains.

A new alternative telephone model was installed in tens of thousands of residences.

Housing construction increased 250% with 39,000 completed residences and 200,000 reparations.

Constructors in the valuta part of the double-economy also made progress. A fifth six-story office building was inaugurated as part of the modern Miramar Trade Centre—located close to several 3-5 star hotels. This joint-venture with an Israeli capitalist Rafi Eitan began in the late 1990s with a projection of 18 six-floor buildings, which would house about 1,000 commercial and office suites. These so-called "intelligent buildings" are 12-15,000 square meters large with all the modern conveniences. None are built until space is bought.

(This joint venture, between Cuba's Cubalse S.A. and Eitan's Grupo BA, reflects interesting contradictions. Cuba supports Palestinians. Eitan was the former head of Mossad's European operations. He was a key responsible behind the bombing of Osirak nuclear plant in Iraq, and the "handler" of Jonathan Polland, convicted of spying on the US for Israel. Today, Eitan is a major landowner in Cuba, a large vegetable and citrus fruit grower, and co-owner of the world's largest citrus juice plant, which uses Cuban citrus. He says everything he has ever done has been as an Israeli patriot. Israel is the only country which consistently backs the US blockade against Cuba.)

Healthcare and education sectors witnessed a leap in new buildings, in repairs and remodeling: 135 large schools and universities, 52 hospitals and 129 polyclinics remodeled; 121 therapy clinics; 400 new ambulances; pharmaceutical industry production growth 26% with 12% more medicines.

Alimentary growth was generalized—examples are: meat, 24%; eggs, 23.5%; yogurt, 13.4%.

In 1989, Cuba imported 94% of its fuel. In 2005, imports were down to 56% consumption as national crude production increased 9.2% over 2004. National oil production had increased six times, from 600,000 to 3.8 million tons, in a decade.

Some of the advances could go unnoticed by people not directly touched by these improvements but all should see that they ate the greater amount of available food and had more appliances to prepare it: 3.1 million new pressure cookers were sold at 140 pesos; 3 million electric plates at 100 pesos, which replace dangerous and smelly gas or alcohol/kerosene cooking plates; millions of rice cookers at 127 pesos; soup and meat cookers at 350 pesos; a simple heating apparatus for bathing in homes without heated water at 20 pesos; 1.2 million fans; color TVs for homes which have poor and energy-demanding sets; replacement of energy-wasteful refrigerators with new thermostats or entirely new Korean-made refrigerators at 3000 pesos on a long time plan.

The government announced that by the end of 2006 all families would have these electric and appliance improvements.

Fidel Castro said that the country had the capacity to provide four times its electricity needs. Sufficient thermo-electric plants were being built or repaired so that blackouts can be avoided.

Many of the nation's youths were being organized to conduct social tasks and save on energy. In 2005, these social workers—mostly university students on study leaves—began going door-to-door replacing filaments and light bulbs with new ones which save enormous amounts of energy and reduce dangerous carbon pollution. The first bulbs are provided courtesy of the government. By the end of the year, five million people had been served. By summer 2006, as predicted, the policy was implemented nationwide, and energy savings alone from the new lights had tripled.

The International Energy Agency reports that the normal high-energy bulbs impact on global warming. Artificial light currently generates nearly two billion tons worth of carbon a year. The IEA states that if low-energy, compact fluorescent lights were used 16 billion tons of carbon would be prevented from polluting the world's atmosphere over the next 25 years.
If US homes switched their five most-used light fittings to energy-saving bulbs, they would save $6 billion and reduce greenhouse gases by half a million tons, reported Andy Smith in "The Independent" (July 3, 06).

In England, reported Smith, low-energy bulbs last six years compared to five months for the polluting ones. That means that the low-energy bulbs cost one-sixtieth the price of higher energy bulbs, given not only the differences in the initial purchase price and electric bills but also the fact that they last 12 times longer.

No other country than Cuba has taken the IEA reports and alarms serious. It is the only country in the world to implement a universal low-energy, low-polluting lighting policy. By summer 2006, the low-energy, low-polluting bulbs are the only ones sold in Cuban stores.

Other social workers were observing and reporting on other electricity wastes, which authorities should attend to. Ironically, the old Soviet magnetic street lighting system was still in place, which has long been wasteful. It is especially an eye-sore now, given the focus on energy saving. Many street lamps remain lit during the day if it is cloudy, but often even with a shinning sun.

Still other social workers were going door-to-door spraying against potential malaria-bearing mosquitoes. The nation had long ago wiped out malaria in this fashion.

Yet another 28,000 social workers were temporarily replacing gasoline station attendants, many of whom were suspected of "diverting" a great deal of gasoline for personal profit. Seventy-two percent of these social workers were women university students.

2005 ended with some setbacks. Due to a decaying water infrastructure and the draught, there was a water supply reduction of 26.7%. Water-carrying trucks were in high demand in many areas.

Havana bus transportation was not better. An alternative transport system was enacted. GETA inspectors stopped near-empty vehicles and asked drivers to take people waiting in line. It was calculated that 60,000 people got rides each day in this cooperative fashion.

There were still many hitch-hikers. Young and pretty women always get rides quickest: most chauffeurs are men. Cubans are not afraid to hitch-hike just as they do not fear walking the streets at night.

As we ate a sumptuous Christmas Eve fish dinner, we debated José Luis Rodríguez' description of 2005. The economy minister closed his long report with the words: "We have initiated a new stage of the Revolution… one of the most fruitful in revolutionary history…We have begun to give real solutions and create conditions which can guarantee overcoming the impediments to consolidating and continuing advancing…with an annual growth rhythm of ten percent," José Luis Rodríguez told the nation.

The parliament designated 2006 as the Year of Saving Energy, and with it came the long-awaited announcement that 15 years of planned and unplanned blackouts would end by the summer, which it did. Actions already taken and others planned could save Cuba as much as 40% wasted consumption while, at the same time, using more electricity.

Cubans heard their government's optimistic plans and promises with hope and skepticism. "We've heard it all before," was a typical head-shaking comment.

Yet there was something different with advances in 2005.

"Despite general dissatisfactions, we are in a much better situation than before 2003," Dr. Omar Everleny, economist at Havana's University's Cuban Economic Studies Centre (CEEC), told me. That was the last year that the "internal dissident" issue was blown up by the US and foreign mass media. Socialism's enemies had renewed predictions that a "free enterprise" system would be attractive to the average Cuban, because people were overtired of economic scarcity, low wages, continued electric blackouts and cut offs of gas and water.

Dr. Everleny had been an economics source for me in the 1990s. He had developed his career and was a frequent writer and lecturer both nationally and abroad. "Wages and pensions have been recently raised significantly, although farmer market food prices are higher than most people's incomes," he said.

Minimum pensions were increased by 50% to 150 pesos; minimum wages from 100 to 225. The medium was 334. The minimum necessary to live on was estimated at 464 pesos, but even with that much many necessary items could not be bought in pesos. For some essentials, people had to pay in *cucs*.

"It is a paradox and hard to understand that nobody can live only on their wages. If people only had their wages, there would be beggars for food on the streets, which is not the case...We calculate that 60% of the people handle convertible currency. For example, most of the merchandise sold across the counter in valuta shops last year—1.5 billion *cucs*—were bought by resident Cubans."

How do so many come by *cucs*?

"There are hundreds of thousands of Cubans working in tourism and joint-venture firms. They get tips and/or supplementary bonuses in *cucs*, although they acquire less now due to the 'Battle of Ideas'," replied Everleny. This "battle" is a reference to government efforts to diminish a growing economic inequality among Cuban workers.

Remittances are also a major source of income. An estimated 1.4 billion US dollars reach about 15% of Cubans in this way, mostly from the US. The Bush government tries to reduce how much can be sent from family members in the US, as it also reduces how often families can visit Cuba. But these prohibitions had not greatly slowed the flow.

"And yes, it is common to steal and accept fencing stolen goods," Everleny lamented, adding, "No one wants to commit suicide."

Many asked why wages were not raised sufficiently so that one can live on them. The economist's response was that to do so would cause inflation and eventually bankrupt the economy. Greater wages must be based upon greater production.

Cuban economists foresee the end of the Special Period within a "short time." While Everleny wouldn't offer a date, the 50th anniversary of the revolution (January 1, 2009) was a hopeful guess.

There were concrete reasons to believe that the only western socialist nation remaining, and the country subjected to the longest blockade by the world's only empire, could pull it off, that it could survive and grow despite the odds.

For the first time in revolutionary history its export-import books were balanced. The approximate seven billion dollars each way was nearly comparable in imports to what it was before the Special Period, in 1989.

What was this due to? Are Cubans super-human, or super-enthusiastic with their leadership and the revolution? Had they hit upon the "correct socialist economic model", as Soviet leaders had maintained that they had?

Everleny believed, like many other Cubans I know, that a key to their tenacious holding out is the personal accountability and political-economic pragmatism persistently exercised by their commander-in-chief. Fidel keeps the people together, in part, by fostering flexibility in economic programming.

In the 1960s, leaders Carlos Rodríquez and Che Guevara pursued two economic courses: state directed capital management and enterprise financial accountability. By 2006, according to Everleny, "there is no one model. We try mixing those two" with sporadic additions."

"I don't know what is theoretically best—but whatever serves the needs of the whole people."

What could put "the very revolution in danger," Minister Rodríguez told the nation, "is thievery and corruption". Rodríguez, and other state leaders, stressed this point during the final 2005 parliamentary session. The state and the Communist party were no longer relying on periodic campaigns to accomplish a severe reduction in such costly immorality, but were relying on the continual "mobilization of our people to confront these phenomena".

Rodríguez projected for 2006 an increase of 72% investments to assure greater recovery. This should include 100,000 residences constructed, three times the number in 2005; 100,000 more telephones in homes; significant increases in sugar and most foodstuffs—18.4% more eggs and 64% more pork, for example—plus total electrification.

Chapter Three:
Tenacious Survival

Tall white flag poles, 138 of them supporting black banners with white star topped by a flame, stand in front of Havana's United States Interests Section office (SINA).

I watched 138 determined Cubans hold as many posters with the photographs of 138 Cuban martyrs. Solemn demonstrators wore T-shirts with the faces of their loved ones.

These murdered Cubans were selected to represent the 3,478 murdered—another 2099 disabled—between 1959 and 2001 by US military and counter-intelligence personnel and their hired guns, Cuban exiles, who want capitalism imposed once again on Cuba. Some of the exiles served prison terms for having invaded Cuba in April 1961—the Bay of Pigs. Many were CIA-trained terrorists, such as Luis Posada Carriles, who told "The New York Times" (July 12-13, 1998):

"The CIA taught us everything, everything. They taught us explosives, how to kill, bomb, trained us in acts of sabotage."

On this very day, February 7, 2006, that Cubans mounted their poignant vigil, the Bush government applied former President Clinton's Helms-Burton law against Mexico. Among other harsh sanctions against Cuba, the law makes it "illegal" for every country in the world to trade or engage in financial exchange with it. So, the Bush regime had a delegation of Cubans dislodged from a Mexico City Sheraton hotel.

At first, even the Yankee-friendly president and foreign minister demanded respect for their nation's sovereignty, as did a unanimous parliament. Bush ignored them and the matter was closed.

United States' immoral, murderous and tortuous actions are against human decency and international laws, yet the responsible international institutions stand by and do nothing.

"How can one not love Cuba and the brave, affable people," I thought as I stood here amongst the roar of hundreds of thousands?

Placards along the *Malecón* sea-wall added to their cry for justice: "We Demand Justice for the Miami Five", "Jail Terrorist Posada", "Fascists—Made in USA" with photos of Bush, Posada, and his accomplice Orlando Bosch. Another showed the faces of Hitler, Bush, Posada and a swastika.

SINA Bush surrogates had installed a rolling red-lettered display of "news" items on the third floor of the borrowed Swiss diplomatic building. As the protest continued, the US flashed its self-righteous contempt for the Cubans that its associates had murdered with the words: "Supposed Cuban martyrs".

During subsequent days of vigilance, SINA "news items" dared to mention Martin Luther King as one of theirs. Bushites had conveniently ignored his roar against their racism, their wars of aggression, their omnipresent exploitation and oppression.

King's wife, Coretta Scott, had just died. In her memory, Alabaman racists—Bush-Christian fundamentalists—burned down nine churches owned and attended by black people.

Another SINA "news item" gloated that Haiti was conducting "democratic elections" in contrast to Cuba. Unmentioned, however, was the February 29, 2004 abduction of the country's democratically elected president, Jean-Bertrand Aristide.

Nor did SINA mention how its "respect for human rights" did not encompass providing housing, education or healthcare for the people, while Cuba was furnishing 70% of the country's heath care by attending poor Haitians with 500 Cuban doctors, medicines and mobile hospitals.

The days following the "free" election, in which the US candidate allegedly won, we watched how "free" the election really was when tens of thousands of ballots for Rene Preval were discovered discarded in trash bins. SINA was silent about this.

Preval was most of the people's favorite since Aristide was not allowed in his country. Opinion polls indicated that Preval would have earned between 60 and 90% of the votes. Eventually, the United Nations commission in Haiti proclaimed Preval the winner.

People stood at the Anti-imperialist Square before the flagpoles for days. Groups of workers condemned the United States for murdering their colleagues.

On February 24, all who had fallen as a consequence of 138 years of struggle for independence were honored at the new *Monte de Banderas* (forest of flags). The 138 martyred representatives had been murdered by hijackers of some 50 Cuban aircraft and boats. It was the same date 111 years before that José Martí initiated the "necessary war" against Spanish colonialism. The 138 years of liberation struggle began in 1868.

Speakers remembered the long history of violent aggression against Cuba, which began in 1959, just months after its liberation victory.

Much of this aggression has been admitted in declassified US government documents.

The CIA shipped in 75 tons of explosives and 45.5 tons of arms in 65 air and sea missions just months before the 1961 Bay of Pigs invasion. Three hundred tons of bombs derailed six trains, caused 150 factory fires and 800 fires in plantations, murdered children in a school and people in market places and cinemas.

This is just the tip of the bloody iceberg of what its trained and equipped agents, such as José Basulto (Brothers to the Rescue), Posada and his buddy Orlando Bosch, had committed. The FBI named Bosch as "Miami's number one terrorist". Nevertheless, President George Bush I pardoned Bosch for his crimes. His son, Jeb Bush, Flordia's governor, pardoned Bosch for illegally entering the US through Florida. Miami made the "mad baby doctor" a city hero.

By 2001, the Cuban government had documented 697 terror actions against Cubans since 1959.

There had been over six *hundred* assassination plans, with many attempts against President Castro.

The most horrendous terrorist action was the Posada-Bosch executed explosion of the Cubana Airlines plane off the coast of Barbados, October 6, 1976. All 73 people aboard were killed, including 57 Cubans—the nation's youth fencing team—11 Guyanese and five Koreans.

On February 24, 1996, Cuba's air force shot down two of six Cessna planes, which the Basulto group had been flying illegally over Havana for months. President Clinton responded by signing into law the terrorist-sponsored, anti-Cuba sovereignty bill by congressmen Helms-Burton.

US government and the mass media ignored the illegality of these repeated over flights—three times on that day alone—and ignored the history of terrorists using such U.S. civilian planes to attack El Salvador, Vietnam and Cuba with bullets, bombs, bacteriological warfare. Also ignored was the fact that the Federal Aviation Administration had earlier that month issued warnings to Basulto pilots against these illegal intrusions.

Basulto received money from CANF to set up his group in 1991. One month before the patient Cuban government decided to stop the pilots' encroachments, on January 20, Basulto told the right-wing newspaper, "El Nuevo Herald": "I was trained as a terrorist by the United States, in the use of violence to achieve goals."

In 1997, CANF-Posada struck again. They launched 13 murderous attacks against tourist hotels.

In May of 2005, Fidel Castro delivered an address at the Anti-imperialist Square about those bombings and the decision to cooperate with the FBI. After many bombings and a murder, SINA chief Michael Kozak finally passed on information about another bomb plan. So, Cuban representatives met the FBI in Havana, June 16-17, 1998.

The US delegation was given documentation, video and audio cassettes of terrorists arrested for placing bombs in hotels. Fidel said there were, "31 terrorist acts and plans against our country. Most of these actions could be traced back to the Cuban-American National Foundation (and the) terrorist network led by Luis Posada Carriles."

US-backed Cuban exiles captured during the Bay of Pigs invasion, April 1961

"The FBI also received recordings of 14 phone conversations from Luis Posada Carriles in which he provided information about terrorist attacks on Cuba. Information was provided on how to locate Posada...FBI agents were also given 60 pages with files on 40 Cuban-born terrorists, most of whom live in Miami, and data on how to find them."

"No terrorist was arrested anywhere, but our comrades were...they were deployed in Miami and were our main source of information about terrorist activities against our country...although, of course, no information had been passed on that would reveal our sources."

The information provided by these brave anti-terrorist activists saved Cuba from scores of planned attacks, so they were arrested on September 12, 1998.

Not surprisingly, to this writer, the FBI deceived the Cuban government, using their information to help trace the patriots.

The FBI informed CANF of their investigation and what charges it would bring even before the courts and public knew about the case. Congressman Lincoln Díaz Balart, whom the FBI confidentially informed, has spoken on Miami television encouraging the murder of Fidel Castro.

Charged with "conspiracy against US national security", the Miami Five spent 17 months in the "hole". They were found guilty, in December, 2001, within minutes after the jury retired from the longest trial in US history.

Gerardo Hernández Nordelo—two life sentences plus 15 years; Ramon Labañino Salazar—life plus 18 years; Antonio Guerrero Rodríguez—life plus 10 years; Fernando González Llort—19 years; René González Sehweret—15 years.

Antonio Guerrero was born in Miami of Cuban parents. After Batista's fall, they returned to Cuba. Years later, Antonio "defected" to Miami and infiltrated terrorist groups. With so much time on his hands while imprisoned, Antonio became a poet. His first book of poetry, "Desde Mi Altura/From My Altitude", was published in 2001 by Editorial José Martí.

Chapter Four:
The Blockade Squeeze

In this world of fast, simple and cheap communication, Cuba is behind and IT costs are higher than anywhere else in the world, to my knowledge. Because of this, my companion in Denmark drew the conclusion that I did not wish to send e-mails to her, perhaps not communicate at all. That was my reading of her message, which I finally was able to see in one of only half-dozen commercial e-mail centers in Havana.

The United States´ punishing blockade is the main reason for the IT difficulties and for our rift.

I had been out of touch with her because I was working in the countryside where no e-mail sites exist. Even in Havana, I didn't e-mail often because there are frequently no connections; when lines are functioning, there are always more customers than machines; besides the wait, the machines operate slowly, making it all the more costly—between $2.50 and $5 minimum fee at the outset.

Telephoning was out of the question since it cost $10 for 100 seconds. Faxing was more expensive.

US hegemony is behind the many embargo laws against Cuba, including the latest which makes it "illegal" for any firm to trade or maintain financial transactions with the "pariah".

Given the nature of competition, not all capitalists cow tow to Washington. A Canadian IT firm offers a compromise—renting the narrowest possible Internet space to Cuba at high rates—so institutions and government offices can buy time on Internet. By then, Cuba had 300,000 e-mails, but if one is a private person, e-mails and Internet access was extremely costly.

This is not because the government wishes to prevent people from access—the few Cubans who seek to overthrow the existing system have ample funds to pay for Internet with their access to US government and its friendly NGOs´ funds, and some also use Havana's US interests office Internet—but because the band is too small and overloaded, and the Canadian company charges a fortune.

The United States has blockaded Cuba since John Kennedy signed the first law in 1961.

On November 8, 2006, the United Nations General Assembly voted against the 45-year old trade embargo/blockade against Cuba. For the 15th year straight, the world's nations urged the US to end the blockade by the largest vote ever: 183 to four. Voting with the United States were Israel, the Marshall Islands, and Palau. Micronesia abstained. Those three countries voting with the US and the one abstention are protectorates of the United States. Four other countries of the 192-nation body were absent. The US methodically ignores the world's assembly's recommendations.

- Cuba estimated, in 2005, that the blockade had cost it $80 billions.
- US's Abbot company must not sell Ritonavir and Lopinavir to Cuba's AIDS patients. Cuba must pay six times Abbot's price elsewhere.
- Medicine helpful to cancer can no longer be bought from Harbison Walker Refractories and some Cuban children must be sent abroad for treatment. The medicine previously bought in Mexico prevented many children from have their limbs amputated.
- US controls firms selling tourist travel over Internet and so it freezes (steals) moneys from such firms as Hola Sun Holidays Limited de Canadá.
- Firms are being fined for trading with Cuba. If a company wishes to continue dealing with the US companies, it must pay the fines and cease trade. The unheard of fine of $100 million is what a Swiss bank must pay (May 2004) for having traded in US dollars with Cuba.
- Individuals and solidarity groups are also fined. Canadian James Sabzali was sentenced to one year in jail and fined $10,000 for selling Cuba a product used to clean drinking water. Members of veteran solidarity groups Venceremos Brigade and Pastors for Peace were fined $1.5 million for acts of "civil disobedience", that is, visiting Cuba. Bush invalidates the constitutional right to travel.

It can't be a total coincidental that when tourist firms are fined for selling tickets to Cuba, they have their offices fire-bombed, as was the case with eight Miami travel bureaus. Cuban hotels were bombed, in 1997, and Spanish and Mexican joint-venture hotel owners were physically threatened.

The anti-Cuba Helms-Burton law is "extra-territorial" and illegal, says the European Union. But it does nothing to anger the "Big One" (Michael Moore's term for the world's empire in his 1996 film with that title).While international political and juridical bodies complain a bit and do nothing, many citizens form solidarity groups (1800 in 128 countries) and act.

There are defiant capitalists who trade with or invest in Cuba and refuse to pay fines. These capitalists lose not only economic possibilities in the US but their owners and directors are denied visas to visit the world's most democratic nation.

Canada's Sherritt International Corporation is one. Viewed as nearly a "hero", Fidel called its directors "courageous" for their "resistance to US aggression."

Sherritt started investing in nickel mining in 1994, and increased nickel-cobalt production from 12 to 22,000 tons in one year. Production is now over 30,000 tons.

Owner Sherritt became a *persona non grata* in the US. It suspended his US subsidiaries. Sherritt then expanded his Cuba businesses into communications, financing, transport, electric plants, real estate, foods and sugar, even vegetables for tourist trade and then tourist hotels. He paid for a trade school and equipment to teach Cuban workers how to use technology unfamiliar to them.

Sherritt started nurturing national crude petroleum (and gas) production. In a decade, it rose from half a million to 3.5 million tons in 2004, 40% of consumption. The firm stands for one-third the national oil production. At-own-risk drilling companies from France, England, Sweden, Spain, Mexico and Brazil are also present.

In the past decade, foreign investments in Cuba have ascended to $30 billion, at an average annual rate increase of 8.2%.

As Bush became more desperate to overthrow the "pariah", Cuba responded by making its own convertible currency (cuc) and removed the US dollar from use. Cubans and travelers experience advantages from this policy. The national peso is strengthened; the penalty risk imposed by the US for dollar usage has diminished; there is an increase of bank accounts in *cucs*; it is simpler for most tourists since they can exchange their own valuta at more places.

Cubans can never rest. Just as they notice a bettering in their economy, the Big One tightens the squeeze. Many feel that the US is preparing to militarily invade. Actions and statements from US leaders indicate this.

Bush instructed his former Secretary of State, Colin Powell, to draw a plan to overthrow the Cuban government and its economy. The May 2004 report led to appropriations for $59 million to "assist a future transition government" complete with its own office and personnel in Washington. Their current plan is to "build solidarity with Cuba's human rights activists"; "give voice to Cuba's independent journalists"; $18 million to keep a C130 in the air sending radio and television signals; $5 million for an advertising campaign against Cuba.

The most absurd double-speak provision is what the future US-backed Cuban government plans to do following its installation. There are reams of proposals on how the new free market economy will function then comes the social programs. Most sardonic is something that not all US children have: free vaccinations. Powell and Bush apparently do not know that Cuban children have had the world's most total health care program since the revolution's beginning.

Bush's previous undersecretary of weapons control, John Bolton, utilized his scant knowledge that Cuba's advanced bio-medical technology system produces and administers 13 vaccines to all children free of charge as "fresh evidence" that Cuba is building mass destructive bacteriological weapons, a lá Saddam Hussein.

The CIA Factbook followed up Bolton's accusation. On its front page on Cuba, one reads that the island is suspected of developing mass destructive bacteriological weapons.

Bolton—a man of such intellect that he proposes the dismantling of the United Nations—was awarded the UN ambassadorship. Bolton and the CIA are classic cases of psychological projection: I do it, so he does it, or he might.

In 1978-9, the US government spread several forms of bacteriological warfare inside Cuba (see my "Backfire: The CIA's Biggest Burn"). These diseases (sugar cane rust, coffee smut, blue tobacco mold, swine fewer, Newcastle disease) destroyed millions of tons of food crops, 500,000 swine and tens of thousands of turkeys.

In 1981, the US government spread bacteriological warfare causing a hemorrhage dengue epidemic, which cost the lives of 158 persons (111 children), and sickened 344,203 people.

Bush's replacement for Powell continued the masquerade. Condoleezza Rice added Cuba to Bush's "evil axis" countries. Besides invaded Iraq, there are six other "evil axis" nations ripe for invasion.

To cover up its own crimes, the US accuses its victim of being the criminal. The question we must ask is, does it get away with it?

Chapter Five:
Enemies of the State

Percy Alvarado is one of the double agents who have infiltrated the Cuban-American National Foundation. CANF leaders Pepe Hernández and Luis Zúñiga (who became George Bush's "human rights" representative in Geneva) directed Alvarado to place bombs in Cuban hotels, and a C-4 bomb in the Tropicana club. Many tourists and dancers would have been murdered. One of them could have been the dancer daughter of my friend, ship Captain Ramón Pérez Miranda.

The men who handed Percy the C-4 material enclosed in plastic shampoo bottles were Luis Posada Carriles and Gaspar Jiménez.

I met with Percy, in February 2006, to discuss his role in the Miami "Non-Governmental Organizations", which funnel US tax dollars to terrorists like Posada and Jiménez, and "dissidents" in Cuba. Alvarado describes these crimes he was ordered to undertake (but did not) in his book, "Confessions of Fraile" (Editorial Capitán San Luis, 2000).

Luckily, Percy was pulled out of the cold by Cuba's Department of State Security (DSE) just one month before the FBI arrested the Miami Five.

"Freedom fighter" Gaspar Jiménez had attempted to murder Fidel Castro, in Venezuela, in 1989. He had already murdered a Cuban fisherman, in Mexico. In 2000, Jiménez, Posada and two other murderers, Pedro Remón Rodríguez and Guillermo Novo Sampoll, tried to murder Fidel again, along with hundreds of students he addressed in Panama. Forty kilos of C-4 were to be placed at the Ibero-American Summit.

Remón had murdered Félix García, Cuba's UN diplomat; Novo was one of the murderers of Chile's ambassador to Washington, Orlando Letelier.

DSE surveillance led to their capture in Panama. In 2001, they were found guilty of some of the crimes they committed or attempted. But the Bush-friendly president pardoned the four multi-murderers in 2005. That is when Posada returned to his CIA home in the US where he was detained not for murder and terror but for "illegal entry".

Under the orders of Hector Pesquera, FBI chief of Miami, all the original files on Posada were destroyed...Panama's legal authorities were trying to collect evidence about Posada's terrorist actions and requested documentation from the FBI.

"New York Times" reporter Ann Louise Bardach, and author of "Cuba Confidential" (2003), told this to Amy Goodman, host of the radio program, "Democracy Now."

Bardach's FBI sources confirmed that: "Sometime after 2002, the evidence in the evidence room of the Miami FBI was destroyed—I understand, shredded... And most courts demand original evidence, not, you know, copies or facsimiles. And somebody made the decision to close the case."

This illegal destruction prevented the most serious charges against Posada from being leveled.

Pesquera was also the in charge of the investigation into who was infiltrating his friends' terrorist organizations in Miami, and this led to the arrest and prosecution of the Cuban Five.

There are many reasons for the CIA and the Bush family to protect these terrorists. One of the key reasons is that some were part of the murder of President John F. Kennedy.

"ZR Rifle, The Plot to Kill Kennedy and Castro", by Claudia Furiati with documentation provided by Cuba´s former chief of state security, General Fabián Escalante (Ocean Press, Australia, 1994), and "Double Cross", a testimonial book by Chicago mafia boss Sam Giancana with his son and grandson, provide the names of conspirators and hit men.

Giancana admitted that he was a JFK murder conspirator. He was also murdered, shortly before he was to testify to a congressional committee investigating the JFK assassination.

Guillermo Novo and Orlando Bosch were among the hit men. Posada provided false papers hoping to cast Lee Harvey Oswald as a Castro agent sent to murder the president. The US congress' 1978 Assassinations Committee called Posada as a witness. It determined that the FBI had turned a blind eye to Posada and other Cuban-American terrorists as suspects. The committee found that the CIA had directed Posada in many terrorist actions, including attempts on Fidel's life.

A 1965 CIA report states that Posada performed "excellently", was "reliable, security conscious".

This is the terrorist whom 1.4 million Havanans demanded be extradited to Venezuela to stand trial during a January 2006 demonstration in front of SINA. US's response was to call Posada an "anti-Castroist", awaiting a final disposition on the "illegal entry matter".

The mass media repeats this status granted Latin America's bin Ladin. CNN, for example, calls him an "extremist anti-Castroist".

The United States has blockaded Cuba since JFK signed the first law. The Bush government has taken the hegemonist step of starting its own Cuban government within the US federal government. This transitory bureau had $59 million at its disposal, in addition to the US Agency for International Development (AID), which has provided another $25 million. The sum for the Cuban Transition Government was increased to $80 million over the following two years.

"Freedom fighting" money goes to US NGOs and others in Europe. They in turn send or hand carry funds to the mercenaries.

CANF is a so-called NGO and a key funding source for Cuban "dissidents", and its paramilitary wings (Cuban National Front and Council for the Freedom of Cuba). US government funding is spent for murderous terror actions.

Bush's earlier SINA director, James Cason, openly organized "dissidents", inviting them not only to SINA headquarters with "open passes" but also to his home residence. They received thousands of radios, tuned to Radio Martí, tape recorders and cameras. SINA's friends sold most of these "presents".

Cason's arrogant stance as a "fighting" diplomat aided in exposing how un-democratic, un-Cuban his "dissidents" were. In December 2002, he told Miami television:

"Every time I go to Miami, I want to meet and have met with all the groups, the Cuban-American National Foundation, the Council of the Freedom of Cuba...The important thing is that the (internal) opposition has to gain ground, because the day is going to come when there is a transition."

When I lived in Cuba, I interviewed some of their mercenaries. One of them was one of Cason's leading "dissidents", Elizardo Sánchez, who traveled without problem from the Cuban authorities wherever he wished. Elizardo and some "poets" and "journalists" I interviewed were emphatic about replacing the Cuban government and economic structure with US-style "democratic" capitalism.

I asked if they could achieve the backing of the majority of their compatriots. They replied that most Cubans were "brain-washed", but with "independent, truthful information" they could be convinced. The sources of "truth" were the US federally funded and directed Radio Martí and NGO publications with material from "independent" journalists in Cuba.

When 75 "dissidents" were arrested, in March 2003, they had $100,000 in cash. Most had no official work but were "employed" to be "dissidents" for the US government and its "NGOs", such as the Republican party's International Republican Institute ($1.7 million that year to provide material support for "democratic activists" in Cuba and to bolster "solidarity committees").

The IRI is just one of scores of NGOs that receive money from AID and its arm the National Endowment for Democracy. The US Chamber of Commerce and the Democratic party also have anti-Cuban NGOs.

In 2003, $100,000 was 2.6 million pesos. That meant that each "dissident" had in cash the equivalent of *five years* wages at the average income.

Of the 75 charged with crimes of sedition, 37 claimed to be "independent journalists". Only four had ever studied journalism and been employed as such. Elizardo Sanchez had appointed one of the actual journalists, Néstor Baguer Sánchez Galarraga, to head *Prensa Independiente de Cuba* and later the *Agencia de Periodistas Independiente de Cuba*.

Like the other "dissidents", Néstor freely used SINA's Internet room to send material to US-backed media: CUBANET, CubaPress, Reporters without Borders. SINA even printed their publication, *La Revista de Cuba*, and distributed it and another, *El Disidente*, through the diplomatic pouch.

Néstor Baguer's testimony—along with ten other double agents posing as "dissidents" (such as Odilia Collazo, president of Pro-Human Rights Party of Cuba, whose main job was to write on "human rights violations" for the State Department, UN's Human Rights Commission, Amnesty International and American Watch)—exposed the 5th column mercenaries.

There was also a great deal of hard evidence presented at the trials. DSE has photographs, videos, audio tapes, original letters (or copies) from known terrorists and CIA agents in Miami and Spain to "dissidents" offering them aid and financing.

The mercenaries were found guilty of "executing an action in the interest of a foreign state with the purpose of harming the independence of the Cuban State or the integrity of its territory", and other crimes of aiding and abetting the enemy—crimes which every government has on its books. They received from six to 28 years in prison.

These sentences created discontent with Cuba, even from some progressive circles, as did the execution of three persons, who had hijacked a small ferry filled with passengers and threatened to kill them with knives and a pistol. These men, with cohorts, hijacked the ferry as the trials against the 75 were underway.

Foreign Minister Felipe Pérez Roque explained why the unusual death penalty was employed: "In the last seven months (of 2003), there have been seven hijackings of Cuban air and sea crafts, encouraged by...the practice of receiving people who use terrorism...to get (to the US)."

Several hijackers, who did make it to the US, were well received and are freely walking the streets.

There had been no death penalty executions since 2000, and other than those three no more as of late 2006.

During my return to Cuba, Captain Miranda and other Cubans told me they are opposed to capital punishment—in fact, a few parliamentarians have voted against it—but that the government's "hard line" has stopped the hijackings. Since the 1997 trials of captured CANF-Posada terrorists no more bombings have occurred. And since the shooting down of intruding pilots, in 1996, Cuba's airwaves have been safe.

Chapter Six:
The Battle for Food

Bill's bicycle whisked through city traffic, mounted the first countryside hill and glided to La Julia in Batabano municipality.

I cycled the 50 kilometers by noon so intent was I on taking a break from noisy Havana and the many Yankee T-shirt-clad unconscionable people. I especially looked forward to revisiting the farm where I had often volunteered in the first half of the 1990s.

GIA-2 was the state collective (*granja*) nomenclature before it became Colonel Mambi Juan Delgado *contingente*, later changed to the José A Fernández UBPC (Basic Units of Production Cooperation) cooperative.

A "Special Period" had been declared by the State soon after the collapse of European state socialism. Cubans lost 63% of their foodstuffs, previously imported from Comecon trade partners. They also lost 85% of export income including oil-for-sugar barter trade. Everybody's belt had to be tightened.

Special Period reforms focused on foreign capital investments and on growing their own food. Volunteers were encouraged to take a leave of absence from city jobs to form contingents of farm workers for a two-year period. About 200,000 people volunteered to supplement traditional farm workers in *granjas*, mainly in Havana province.

Their fine patriotic spirit was seldom matched with efficient skill. While production increased at many of these contingent-worked *granjas*, production costs were often three times more than income. Harvests still accounted for only one-fourth consumption. Cuba could not afford such great amounts of imports.

In 1993, Defense Minister Raúl Castro said that the Farming Production Cooperatives (CPA) were six times more effective than the state collectives. CPAs were formed in the 1960s as cooperatives of private farmers, owners and usufructaries. Members share in profits from sales and can hire day laborers at peak times. State farm workers received fix wages regardless of production quantity or quality. Raúl proposed that most of the *granjas*, which held 80% of agricultural lands (four million hectars), be transformed into new usufruct cooperatives with some CPA benefits.

UBPC were then established. They were to be cost-accountable, profitable enterprises. Workers were to have usufruct rights to the land with some worker decision-making. This should include some products to sow and elections of leaders (instead of being appointed by the state), who were subject to recall. Workers were to be further stimulated to stay on the land with the offer of housing to be constructed nearby, with better wages and plots for self-consumption. But there would be no profit-sharing, yet.

Manuel farm labour with ox.
Photo: Cuban Organic Support Group, England

Most contingent members returned to their waiting city jobs. Those few who did remain on the restructured farms were joined by traditional collective farm workers and other country folk from eastern provinces.

Hungry farmers milled before the camp kitchen. Benito, the tall lanky Microjet drummer, approached me. Microjet was the irrigating system—hoses fixed in the air or on the ground from which a fine spray of water is projected. Benito had been a contingent member, who had formed the Microjet band with other volunteers. "The Microjets are gone, Ron. I'm the only one remaining. But others you knew are still here and most have their houses. I'm way down on the list since I am single. But Edgardo and Guillermina got theirs.

"The camp is improved. We are fewer here now so we can share a room with only one person instead of six. And we got rid of that fucking sex restriction. Now we can have a woman in bed."

I biked the kilometer to the concrete-block housing compound, which I witnessed started with four houses. As I gazed at the identical grey structures, a woman walked out of one. Despite her *sombrero*, I recognized the muscular Guillermina Montero. After embracing, we walked into her house to see her husband, Edgardo Rochet. They insisted I stay for lunch.

Most of those who have their own houses no longer eat at the camp cafeteria. If they do, a meal costs 50 centavos. Home-owners prefer to buy their food and eat at home.

Guillermina and Edgardo showed me their home and insisted I stay with them. They have plenty of space: four rooms, bathroom and kitchen. Since they live alone, one room is used to store fresh harvested foods and three unused bicycles, all lacking tires and tubes, "which cannot be found", lamented Edgardo.

Their kitchen is charred black from an accident with the kerosene cooking apparatus.

"We should use gas but it is not as available as is kerosene. We are all to get the new electric plates this month, and then I'll `find´ some paint to brighten up the kitchen," Edgardo said.

"The state says it will be making refrigerators available to us also," interjected Guillermina enthusiastically. "We haven't had one for years since ours broke down and there were no parts."

The bathroom light burns constantly because of a broken fixture, which will soon be replaced with the new energy-saving filaments and bulbs. The sink is broken. More often than not there is no running water for showering or flushing the toilet. Buckets are kept filled for both functions. The residential compound gets its water from the well at the nearby

A new farmer's market.
Photo: Cuban Organic Support Group

countryside school, but there are no set times for water flow. Since many of the couples both work, it is often a house-wife neighbour who fills up empty buckets for others.

The living room is the centre of attention, because of the Chinese Atec-Panda television set, which Guillermina "won" for being voted *destacada* (distinguished) worker many times. She is paying half price (4000 pesos) on a three-year time plan without interest. Her average wage is 500 pesos a month, which supplements her 262-peso retirement. Guillermina retired last year. At 56, she is the oldest woman worker.

"I like to work and helping out the banana plantation crews, plus we put away a little extra for some future event," the broad-faced woman said, showing youthful white teeth. After lunch, she returned to her bananas.

"Now, that we have specific work responsibilities, I've decided to take the afternoon off. I'm caught up with weeding our papayas," explained Edgardo. He wanted to talk with me while cleaning house and preparing for dinner.

Edgardo, 50, gets 700 pesos monthly. These "wages" are advances based upon the previous year's income. The crews earn according to the product results they cultivate. All workers spend some time on the *libreta* (rations) crops like potatoes plus their own designated crops.

At the end of each season, sales are divided amongst the workers after the cooperative takes its cut for maintenance, administration and new investments. Last year, Edgardo earned 8000 pesos over the advance monthly "wage". Workers in the more demanding guayaba fruit plantation earned twice that. Some crops require less work and bring in less income.

"We can feel the differences, Ron. We are more comfortable since share-profiting was introduced and since we got our house, in 1997. We're earning three times what we did when you were here. We pay a pittance for the house until we own it outright (they can't be thrown out by law), and nothing for gas, water or electricity.

"Of course, not all is roses. They didn't come near their promise of housing construction and we still don't have more say running things but the system is more open. So I decided to join the party. I'm now a militant."

Guillermina came in with a small chicken in one hand and a bottle of my name in the other. She had taken off work early to buy her favorite meat at 60 pesos, and a cheap rum at 30 pesos.

"We celebrate your return, Ron. Cheers," and we downed a tingling shot.

Guillermina caressed our dinner with a large callused hand. Its eyes closed peacefully and she twisted its neck in one motion. Not a pip. It took Guillermina just minutes to pluck and cut up the chicken. As it simmered in a pan, and as the sweet potatoes, rice and beans were cooking—which Edgardo had prepared along with a fresh green and tomato salad—the loving couple took a bucket bath together. Edgardo had heated the water with a Chinese spiral electrical heater.

Dinner was delicious and festive.

My hosts' home-town baseball team and a Havana club were starting a three-game series, which must be seen. After the Walt Disney cultural imperialism hour, we watched the game on their 101-channel television set, which receives only the five Cuban stations. Just five of the 23 families in this compound have TV sets so several neighbors roared or moaned with us.

Dwarf banana plantation.
Photo: Cuban Organic Support Group

Chapter Seven:
Life on the Farm

Grunting pig, crowing cock, buzzing mosquito, child crying—you name the noise and it penetrates through wood-slatted windows that can't be shut tightly and through the porous concrete structure. I rose from the narrow cot and thin mattress and stepped into the acrid bathroom. Coffee and a plain hard bun and we were all but ready to start the work day. But not before filing sharp my 40-cm long banana machete, Guillermina's knife and Edgardo's heavy hoe.

Entering the mature plantation in the early morning dew is a venerate experience. The shadowy silence and fresh moisture embraces and comforts. Under the tall fruit banana and shorter burro banana trees, the sun does not penetrate to human height and fronds protect one from rain. All is green and tranquil.

This was my experience again, just as I described it a dozen years ago when Guillermina and I worked the fruit jungle. Today, Guillermina works in the largest of two banana plantations with 54,000 trees, divided into 12 sections. One worker is responsible for each plot of some 4,500 fruit-bearing plants, but they often work in pairs or small groups.

GIA-2—still its common name—has fewer bananas than when it encompassed 900 hectares. All UBPCs were reduced in size so that the fewer workers could better grasp the tasks. Much time was lost when the land was so vast and the 300 workers had to walk so long to and from work. GIA-2 split into four UBPCs. This one of 192 hectares is tilled by 126 workers.

Guillermina introduced me to fellow workers as "*uno cubano más*" (just one more Cuban), making me blush with pride.

Today, we were to cut dried ends of the long fronds before the trees grew over our reach, and the outer layer of the trunk, the *yagua*, behind which thrives a little green frog. This cute, gentle animal unintentionally causes fright in most Cuban women and some men. Even "superwoman" Guillermina gives a yelp and takes a step back upon seeing one. So, men usually cut the *yagua*.

Stooping and slashing round the plant, stepping to the next, stooping and slashing, simultaneously swatting mosquitoes and mites. That's the routine but it doesn't need to be boring. We are our own bosses, in part, and can stop when we want, chat when we wish, or exchange tasks.

Lunch at the cafeteria was tasty and nourishing but some of the old timers reminded me that when all 300 workers lived in the camp, instead of 46 now, the meals were richer. There is almost never fish—Cuba's fishing fleet had been drastically reduced—and never beef. True, but now they have more variety of vegetables and fruits, because they have diversified their crops.

The topic of food is more troublesome to camp dwellers than is camp cleanliness, including toilet-shower hygiene. The facilities have deteriorated. There are no lights; fixtures are broken and all bulbs burnt or stolen. Only two showers function and must be alternately shared by men and women. Plumbing is worse: only four clothes washing sinks work; "toilets" are still holes in the ground with soiled newspapers beside them.

After lunch, I was shown the cooperative's biggest challenge: grape growing. A Spanish wine growing investor imported thousands of young plants. Under his instructions, workers fastened vines between three wires stretched over hundreds of posts. Grapes require intensive labour: constant watering, stem cutting and lots of weeding.

They have sown peppers between the 500 rows containing 37,000 grape vines.

Thirty thousand papayas have been planted behind the grapes. Farm administrators bought seeds from private farmers for the first crop and hope to use their own seeds for the next planting. Digging holes in the hard red earth is arduous "man's work". As we hack, women unload 6,000 new plants from a borrowed oxen cart. (They used to have their own oxen but sold them to buy tractors.) Plants are then placed in holes, which once contained other papaya plants that died from lack of proper planting and inadequate irrigation.

Mirta, yet another member from Santiago de Cuba, complains of the needless loss.

"The field director neglected to see to it that the earth was properly watered and fertilized before he ordered us to rush the planting."

Why didn't you say so?

"Ah, what good does complaining do," she retorts, her eyes rolling.

"We have complained about some things," added her partner, "like the ridiculous guard duty. We work six days a week and half-day every other Sunday. On top of that, we must conduct four monthly 12-hour night shifts `guarding´ the fields. But we cannot be armed while the thieves may be. They are prepared to come in the steal of the night and take crops without our seeing them, or if we do, so what. What can we do to stop them?"

Many years ago, worker-guards were armed with shotguns but when a young thief was shot and killed local people protested and the guns were removed. Sometimes it does pay to complain.

Night guarding, however, is a condition of membership, these workers say. The response to earlier protests was: guard duty or dismissal.

Later, I spoke with an older man whose full-time job is to guard an abandoned resident shelter. He lives alone in one of the run-down shacks on 225 pesos a month. There is no electricity or running water. His prepared meals are delivered to him.

"You know us Cubans. Without a guard, every bit of concrete left would be broken up and hauled off. They say they will rebuild this place one day for residences. What do I know?" he shrugged.

General Assembly Democracy

After dinner, most of members attended the monthly general assembly in which evaluations are made and plans laid. The UBPC director, Matías Cabrera, was appointed by the regional UBPC firm three years ago to replace a negligent leadership, which involved some fraud. Matías, 40, had been a farm worker since youth.

Matías opened the meeting with the accountant's financial report: no loses in three years; monthly profit sharing is above average in last period at 125 pesos; our sales, especially to tourist centers, assure us profit, and we are regularly paying off our 2.2 million debt; cafeteria is operating at a loss—each meal costs thrice what camp residents pay: 60 pesos monthly.

There were no questions or comments.

Then Matías delineated problems and plans in a monologue stream.

"We have not received sufficient boots but more are expected; we have problems with our irrigation system and this is acute, especially for avocados; we are replacing the lost papayas.

"Thirty-one members are behind in paying their union dues, including some leaders. This shows a lack of respect. There were 29 departures in December—four firings: 2 for thievery, 2 for indiscipline and disorderly drunkenness; the remainder decided to quit.

"Camp discipline is faulty and the grounds are dirty. The cafeteria lacks some essentials. Since we do not foresee enough housing construction in the near future, I am proposing that the camp be legalized as permanent residences for each person or couple without a home and installed with cooking facilities. In this way, we can close the cafeteria and everyone will have a home.

"From now on, fines will be levied for those who do not clean their area adequately. There are 15 undocumented workers. If they do not get their papers in order within a week, they are dismissed. The administration is responsible and would be required to pay a penalty. Beginning tomorrow all workers are required to participate in potato weeding."

"That is all. Are there any questions or comments?"

Only one man spoke. He asked why they didn't buy sufficient papaya plants to replace the loss.

Matías replied that there were not enough funds and they must now concentrate on potatoes.

After the rather dry assembly, I milled about outside with some long-faced members. People were unhappy with the constant turn-over of members, with the fines imposed for untidiness, and Matías' manner of addressing them as underlings.

Mirta and her crew said that they didn't speak up because, "it would not change anything."

Edgardo and others said that the promises of elections and worker decision-making exist only on paper. Young Alejandro, a recent member, also from Santiago and known as the leading *jodedor* (clownish joker) viewed it differently.

"I see no need to criticize or rebel. We take orders, because we know the leaders want to go forward for and with us. They are *mamé*" (little mangoes, meaning good people).

Chapter Eight:
Feeding a Nation

We walked directly from breakfast to the fields. The *matutino* (morning meeting) is no longer a cooperative feature, discarded as a "waste of time".

Several scores of hectares with rows half-a-kilometer long, each with about 1,500 potato plants and tens of thousands of choking weeds. This is not a pleasant sight. No one looks forward to work today and the coming days it will take to hack and pull up weeds.

Mild-mannered Alex, the production chief, and Juan, potato crew leader, led us into the first rows. They demonstrated how to hoe the weeds without getting too close to the plants. The problem is that to avoid cutting potatoes one must stoop over most plants to pull out the weeds growing amidst the plants themselves.

A thorough job of weeding required much more time and painful stooping than the majority were prepared to offer. Most hacked the weeds without getting down to the roots, and the amount of stooping to pick out weeds that can not be hoed was not commensurate with the amount of weeds.

Hacking, stooping, hacking and stooping. My head ticked with figures. How many rows, potatoes, weeds, how many man/woman hours? I came up with some three million potato plants. And they should cultivate twice in the season. So there must be two campaigns with most members participating.

Alex realized that the work was so tedious and took so many days that he did not conduct quality control.

Juan showed me their use of biological control against pests. The ladybug eats the bigger bad guys, *cinche*. Juan said that most farmers are using as many ecological methods of farming as possible. State instructions and propaganda portraying the worthy of organic over chemical had ensured that awareness to the fact has risen greatly.

"The only problem," Alex said, "is if the good bugs get overwhelmed by the bad ones and can't reverse their growth. If a plague sets in then we must use chemical pesticides. The problem with that is once they are used it takes a long time for the poison to disappear so that we can go back to biological control. In the five years I've been here we've used chemicals just two or three times. We can't be completely ecological. Our priority is to put enough food on everybody's table and, hopefully, without having to use precious valuta to import it."

Farming Structures[1]

All farmers are required to grow and sell basic products to the state, in order to assure everyone rationed goods at subsidized prices, the libreta, and at less subsidized prices on the state farm markets, set up in 1994 to compete with and undersell the supply-demand farmer markets.

At first, private farmers supplied most of the goods but at prices few could afford. Soon state cooperative farmers began selling products at cost+ prices after meeting libreta commitments. The army, which produces much of its own food, joined in the competition with its EJT soldier-farmers.

Private farmers are still entitled to own up to 65 hectares of land. There are only a few thousand individual farmers remaining, who are not part of a cooperative. In the 1960s, most independent and cooperative farmers created the National Association of Small Farmers (ANAP) to represent them before the state. In the 1990s, ANAP set up a new organization for mutual financial benefit, the Credit and Service Cooperatives (CSC).

In 2005, ANAP farmers produced 60% of the nation's root and green vegetables and grains, 60% of its pork, and was the major producer of tobacco, livestock, fruits and coffee. It is especially CCS farmers who earn the greatest valuta profits from Cuba's renowned cigars and coffee.

The state collectives had produced practically all the sugar and rice. But the UBPCs now produce 90% of the sugar, and it is also a major producer of green and root vegetables and fruits.

Most rice is produced by yet another form of farming: the Urban Truck Farms. The UTFs are tilled by family units and some full-time city farmers, who utilize organic intensive growing methods. They grow the best green vegetables, herbs and condiments.

UBPCs now till about half the nation's soil, double what they had in 1995. ANAP's 300,000 members till approximately 35% of the cultivated land (25% of total agricultural lands); the EJT about 8%; some old granjas still exist and till about 8% of the land. These farm workers now have better wages and some profit-sharing. They cultivate some vegetables but mainly citrus fruits. The remainder of produce comes from the UTFs, which includes self-consumption and market sales.

There are over one million farmers of all kinds. This is 21% of Cuba's 4.6 million workers (service=64%, industry=14%). No farm worker any longer lives only on wages. Profit-sharing has taken over and has satisfied a basic demand.

These changes have also improved the state budget. Subsidization of agriculture has decreased significantly—from 54% in the 1990s to 20% today (2005).

Dr. Santiago Rodríguez Castellón, agricultural economist at Havana University's Cuban Economic Studies Center (CEEC), provided facts and figures and described changes.

"The reduction of subsidization is one of our greatest achievements. Another is the 50% increase of all vegetables in the last three years. We now produce 60% of our food, up 220% from a decade ago. We are not long from when the Special Period will be concluded."

Inventive farmers revert to ploughing with oxen when the collapse of the Soviet Union, combined with the US blockade, left Cuba without fuel for its tractors

There is yet a ways to go, Dr. Rodríguez admits. "It had been predicted that UBPCs would take over all *granja* lands and that all would be profitable. While they have *doubled* production, only half are profitable; others must rely on state subsidies and credits.

"Not nearly as many housing units have been built as promised. Many leave UBPCs because they must live in cramped collective compounds. The longer established private cooperatives are more attractive. The few *granjas* left are still too dependent on the state and lack many resources. Moreover, poor work habits inherited from before the Special Period have not been eradicated."

The economist lamented that the UBPCs "have not matured to the point where workers elect their own leadership, in most cases. The objective of autonomy is still extant, but it is difficult to define and separate where the state stops and the cooperative autonomy process starts. The old centralism, however, has been broken."

It was the state's top leadership, which took the initiative to combat, what many call, "revolutionary paternalism".

Director Matías

Matías' house looks like Edgardo-Guillermina's. The key difference is that he has DVD and other modern entertainment technology, which attracts neighbors. They come to borrow salt or sugar; some stay to watch TV and drink coffee, which his young wife gladly serves.

Matías is not preoccupied with critical questions posed.

"Membership turn-over is not a problem. There are always more seeking work than leave. Those who leave don't want to work hard. Too many Cubans are spoiled and lack consciousness. And we do have a stable group of 78 workers—mainly those who have housing."

What about the papaya crop?

"The original planting was faulty, a lack of consciousness again. Sure, I have enough money to buy the necessary plants but I didn't want to tell the assembly this. They must concentrate on potatoes now."

Lying for convenience is not viewed culturally as a "sin" or wrong, especially if the intention is well meant.

Does his leadership style turn people away?

"Look who's in my house? Everyday it is like this, a dozen or more people pass in and out. Some may not like it when I'm precise. But they can't deny the facts: we have had a profit each year I've been here; most weeds get removed; we've made several million peso investments in the best paying crops: avocados, papayas, mangoes, guayaba, and the wine grapes, which is a long-term investment."

Matías may only receive a fixed monthly salary of 500 pesos, but some workers point out that he gets shares based upon their production, has the only house in the compound with a freezer, and has several rice cookers plus the entertainment apparatuses, which many enjoy.

Chapter Nine:
From Farm to Table

When I worked as a volunteer in agriculture in the 1990s, one of the greatest problems was the distribution system. The December 1993 national assembly sessions included an alimentary report by Candido Palmero, former head of agricultural contingents. He said that the contingents and the new cooperative UBPCs could guarantee their production goals but he couldn't guarantee that "you will eat all harvested crops, because we don't have our own trucks to distribute goods."

Candido considered the state centralized food distribution centers, Acopio, a disaster! "We recommend that farm workers have the responsibility, authority and means to do the entire job, from breaking ground to delivery."

Although Fidel and other state leaders expressed interest in changing the system and distributing directly to local markets, there remains much to be done. In contrast to then, however, other forms of distribution are allowed. For example, most ANAP (National Association of Small Farmers)

Intensive organic farming in a Havana mental health garden. Cuba is first in world with ecological cultivation.
Photo: Cuban Organic Support Group

cooperatives have converted to the Credit and Service Cooperative (CCS), which own and share farm equipment, and many own their own distribution trucks, a significant advantage over most state cooperatives.

Most private producers distribute directly to designated farmers markets, but they must purchase gasoline and parts in the convertible currency. If they distribute their own crops, they also lose precious time from the fields or they must employ drivers and (illegally) vendors.

Nevertheless, direct distribution to market places, in 2006, was common fare for 25,000 individual farmers, for nearly 2000 CCSs and the remaining 750 Agricultural Production Cooperatives (CPAs), and the farmer-soldier EJT. Even a few profitable UBPCs and granjas_have sufficient funds to buy vehicles and distribute directly to markets, or they set up stands where people can buy those products remaining after sales to the state.

Distribution and Investigative Journalism

Matías Cabrera did not see any problem with the traditional Acopio system.

"Improvements have occurred since your time. Both producers and distributors are better in advising one another concerning times of harvest, how much shall be collected and what days the trucks will arrive," the UBPC farm director told me.

"We get three different prices for our products—one for the libreta rations, another for the state controlled farm markets, and a third from the tourist hotels. The Acopio collects and distributes more exactly.

"Thievery of our products is prevented because a farmer rides in the trucks. He observes what is delivered where and sees that the correct payment is noted. Control is better."

In February 2006, the Communist party newspaper, "Granma", conducted an unusually critical investigative series about problems in agriculture, farm markets and distribution. "Granma" confronted distribution problems, which Matías apparently oversaw, when it interviewed the Acopios national leader, Frank Castaneda Santalla.

"We recognize that our transportation is deteriorated. Four hundred trucks are inactive for lack of parts and repairs. We have 1,200 trucks for the whole country, and only 60% are active. The Ministry of Agriculture has recently invested funds in tires and batteries, in order to reactivate 172 trucks and 92 trailers. Most of our trucks are from the old socialist Europe. They have 20 years or more of use and consume enormous amounts of fuel."

Acopios also had problems with too few front line employees.

"We have 17,000 employees...but 40% are administrators and bureaucrats. We propose to reduce them by fifty percent."

Castaneda added that Acopio workers needed better wages and an improved image. Both Castaneda and Vice-Minister of Agriculture Juan Pérez Lamas, whom "Granma" also interviewed, maintain that the chief cause of insufficient foodstuffs is not with Acopio distribution weakness, however, but lays in insufficient production.

Castaneda said that illegal distribution intermediaries would disappear if farmers were motivated to produce more, if they would be content, "to live on the income from their harvests and not motivated to sell at higher prices."

In "Granma's" February 21 article, Ciego de Ávila province Acopio leader, Giuvel Rodríguez Rivero, contradicted Castaneda and Pérez.

"The distribution of agricultural products is an old challenge, which has not been totally solved. The principal problem is lack of transport," he said.

"I am of the opinion that the Acopio is not serious. It does not comply with its commitments, and should be more flexible in ratifying sowing (and harvest) plans exactly. And when the Acopio delays in collecting harvests, they are sold to whomever appears. Is this not an illegality? I won't deny it (but in this way] the harvests are not lost. We know there are receptive stomachs."

In another "Granma" interview, ANAP's president, Orlando Lugo Fonte, who is a member of the State Council, offered a frank portrayal of problems: contractual agreements often not made or completed, lack of packaging causing loss of "much food harvested", and lack of weights where crops are delivered at the Acopios.

"There are very few animal weights so their weight is estimated by a functionary; and there are too few weights at farmer markets. Another major problem for farmers is late payment of delivered crops by the ministries of agricultural and sugar.

"Ministry functionaries are often undisciplined in setting prices in time for farmers to buy seed. And the ministries buy products at different prices based on quality. But in most markets, the sellers do not make quality distinctions in sale prices. Farmers must also pay 29% of the product price for distribution and commercialization," Lugo explained.

Sometimes farmers' income did not meet their costs.

Lugo said that the more expensive supply-demand farmer markets are often supplied by self-employed intermediaries. They usually drive to the fields and buy products directly from farmers. And there is less control in these markets, including veterinary certificates, than in the state-run markets, where prices are set by the state and quality checks are made by inspectors.

"Granma´s" interview with Vice-Minister Pérez focused on food marketing and common complaints of high food prices. Pérez, a former farmer, offered the following figures: each person has a monthly need of 30 pounds of all forms of vegetables, grains and fruits, requiring 2.5 million tons. Another 2.5 million tons are produced for food consumption outside the home—restaurants, tourist centers, hospitals, canned goods for export.

Seventy percent of household foodstuff was sold in the state's 13,800 free markets. In addition, there were 400 small organic food stands where prices were often arbitrarily set.

"Granma" asked the vice-minister why prices are often arbitrarily established, why payments are late, and why farmers often end up on the short end of the stick.

"We are strengthening the Acopios...We make imprecise estimates of harvests and this results in inadequate control in the organization of packing and transportation...We have made up for most back payments and this problem should disappear."

According to Acopio leader Castaneda, the Acopios lacked at least 6,000 scales. Regarding the lack of weighing products, Pérez simply admitted that this occurs.

Pérez added that there is still a scarcity of means of production and seeds to meet all farmers' needs. Many types of seeds were sold to farmers at subsidized prices. However, the state could not provide sufficient fertilization, so what there was, was sold to the highest yielding farmers.

Nevertheless, "farmers receive more resources than before: modern irrigation technology (for some farms), using less fuel and more electricity, and there are more tractors and oxen than before the special period. But we lack work clothing, boots, machetes and sharpening files, tractor parts and tires...We deal out to the best producers...no type of farmer is discriminated against. All farmers get free technical advice from state institutions."

"Our biggest challenge is to reduce the high prices. To do so we must achieve greater production."

Other problems included, "Undisciplined functionaries, and intermediaries who live off the sweet of the workers, which has to do with our lack of control in the ministry. We must confront the irresponsible ones."

Despite the many problems, the latest Special Period alimentary reforms had definitely advanced the battle for food. The state had increased its prices for farm products—up to five times the value in five years. Individual and cooperative private farmers were assured continued ownership of their lands by new recruitment. Many of the younger generation, which had left their family farms, had returned, and other youths, including women, had become farmers. Private farmers were assured profitable commercialization by employing accountants and technicians.

While the quantity and quality of produce had greatly improved, the reforms had led to the introduction of a petty bourgeoisie and a small exploited farm proletariat, allowing some private farmers and the illegal wholesale intermediaries to live far above median standards. They form part of the "new rich", which the state combats in its "Battle of Ideas" morality propaganda campaign .

State collective farm market in Havana.
Photo: Cuban Organic Support Group

Chapter Ten:
On the Market

"They pay us in script, which we can only spend in the company store to which we owe our soul," just like in Tennessee Ernie Ford's song.

That was a bitter refrain from an old friend and political refugee, who, in 2006, had lived in Cuba nearly three decades. Bill referred to the fact that most Cubans' income is only in the national peso, which can not be used anywhere else in the world, nor can the convertible currency. Everyone can use *cucs* to buy many products, including essential ones, that can't be bought in pesos.

This description of food marketing is what I saw in 2006.

Acquiring food in Cuba is quite special. Some food is nearly a birthright "taken" for a pittance on the *libreta*—heavily subsidized items available on one's ration card. And then there are those items one must buy on the free farmers' markets, of which there are at least three types:

Agropecuarios—state controlled markets with maximum (*topados*) prices; these account for 70% of national market sales;

Agromercados—supply-demand markets established in 1994 and supplied mainly by the private farmers and their cooperatives (ANAP); prices are 40% higher, overall, than *agropecuarios*.

Agricultural urbana—the urban truck farms, which sell produce at high prices at roadside stands.

The UTCs produced 4.1 million tons of ecological vegetables and condiments, in 2005. Most produce goes to self-consumption for the city family growers at cost.

Not only Bill wants an end to the *libreta*, so do many of the well-off Cubans, including economist Omar Everleny. He said that many Cubans sell items not needed at high prices to others. In this way, the state was wasting funds subsidizing some people unnecessarily. Others are worried that without the *libreta* they will not have enough money to buy many essential items. The state instituted rations when the US started its blockade so that no one goes hungry. Everleny proposes that those with low incomes be subsidized with cash to buy these goods on the open markets.

What is available on rations costs an adult about 35 pesos a month. I calculated that to acquire these goods on the free markets would cost four to five times that amount. Bear in mind that the average wage is 334 pesos, the minimum 225, and minimum pension is 150. Economists estimate that the minimum wage must be doubled, in order that each person can buy the current monthly consumption of 30 pounds of vegetables, fruits and grains, plus some meat.

Libreta goods available monthly per person for 2005-6, followed by what was available in 1994-5

Sugar	= 5 pounds (lb) in relation to 6 lb
Salt	= small portion both periods
Rice	= 7 lb to 6 lb
Beans	= 1 lb to 1.25 lb
Potatoes	= 2-3 lb to rarely
Grains	= ½lb to ?
Ground beef	= to ¾ lb
Chicken	= 1/4 chicken to 1 lb for children only
Fish	= ½ small fish sometimes to the same
Eggs	= 6-8 to 14
Coffee	= ½ lb pure to ¼ lb pea mix
Cacao	= ½ lb to 0
Powdered milk	= ½ lt. For children up to 7 and then ½ lt. Soya to 1 lt. Up to age 7
Vegetables	= 0 to a few sometimes
Bread	= 1 roll per day to the same
Tooth paste	= 2 tubes per persons to 1 tube per sometimes
Cooking oil	= 0 to ½ lt. Sometimes
Hand soap	= 1 sometimes to 1 rarely
Laundry soap	= 0 to rarely
Detergent	= 0 to rarely
Cigars	= 4-6 to 6
Cigarettes	= 6 packs to the same
Matches	= 1 little box to the same
Rum	= 1 cheap bottle sometimes to the same
Clothing and shoes	= 0 to officially each year but not always: 1 pants, 1 dress, 1 shirt or blouse, 4 underwear, 1 shoes/boots

Farmer Markets

Everyone must buy some foods at the markets. Since I lived just behind Havana's best stocked *agromercado* (at 19th between A & B), I shopped there my first week until a vendor refused to see my point that wearing a US flag T-shirt was supporting propaganda against his own people. I then shopped mainly at the army's EJT market several blocks away. Shopping prices were:

ITEM	Agromercado	Agropecuario
Root vegetables	3-5 pesos lb	1-5 pesos; potatoes 2 lb
Tomatoes	5 lb	1-2 lb
Lettuce, cabbage	5 per	2-3 per
Peppers	8 per	5 per
Garlic	4 per bunch	3 per
Onions	10 per bunch	5 per
Rice	4 lb	3-3.5 lb
Beans	8-10 lb	7-8 lb
Oranges	1 per	by lb or ? .50 per
Grapefruit	2 per	by lb or ? 1 per
Papaya	5 per	1.5 lb or 3 per
Pineapple	10-20 per	5-7 per
Fruit bananas	1 per	by lb or ? .50 per

Beef is not sold in pesos. If someone slaughters a cow illegally, there is a stiff prison term. Cattle are reserved for milk and bulls for farm work, plus some sales only in *cucs*. Since everyone must exchange hard currencies into *cucs*, the state obtains currency it can use for imports.

Cubans buy undergarments and new clothing in *cucs* or they come from families living abroad. The numerable *cuc* markets, cafes and restaurants charge about the same prices or even more than in the First World. A litre of juice, for example, can be two or three *cucs*. Eggs cost .15 each; a pound of beef 6; an apple .50; a good rum anywhere from 5 to 15—equivalent to a month's minimum wage or more in pesos.

Cubans buy popsicles sold from state-run refrigerated bell-ringing trucks at five pesos. Many buy a dry ham sandwich at many peso or convertible currency stands for the equivalent of one or more day's wage. And at the peso stands, one must stand to down the snack in a flash.

Pork can be bought at most forms of markets in pesos. The supply-demand markets have been forced to cut prices from 55 to 65 pesos a pound to 35 to 50, because the state is a sharp competitor now. State collectives, some cooperatives and the EJT sell pork for between 25 and 40 pesos.

Hygiene at farmers markets is not optimal. There is insufficient refrigeration so meat is laid in the open so customers can see what is offered and flies can eat. Sales clerks handle the meat with ungloved hands, which are also used to handle dirty bills.

There are more garbage containers in much of Havana than a decade ago, and collection is more regular. But there are too few containers or none in many districts. And some are stolen to be used elsewhere. People are accustomed to throwing trash, bottles and cans anywhere it fancies them.

While the state no longer can guarantee all foods and clothing in pesos, it does sell recycled clothing. Used clothing were being sold for 30-50 pesos for pants; 15-20 for shorts; 25-30 for shirts and blouses; 40-80 for dresses; 40-50 for light jackets.

An average family uses about 35-45 pesos a month for electricity, cooking gas and alcohol, water and telephone, for those who have the latter. The long-maintained monthly price of 19 pesos for 150KW was increased to 26 at the start of 2006. And there is a graduated price rise for greater usage. If one uses as much as 300KW, for example, it costs 91 pesos.

Many complained about the electricity increases; the state countered with a savings campaign. Besides the many programs underway, one could learn to simply turn off light switches, TVs and radios when not in use. But that is a strong challenge to the lackadaisical part of Cuban culture.

Chapter Eleven:
A Farewell to Farms

"We have greater stability in this camp and people work hard. They feel tranquil and earn well," commented, Luis Enrique, the director of El Rubio

I was on a visit to the smallest of the UBPCs, which had split off from the José A Fernández original cooperative. Its campsite lays two kilometers away from it. I spoke with a handful of the 60 workers, in order to get a cursory idea of how conditions are for them, and how they tackle decision-making. Most of them had come from the eastern provinces but, they said, there is little turnover and no thievery. Their director is a young man, recently promoted from production chief.

The state had not built any housing for these workers, and only six at the other two farms, which had once formed the original UBPC. So the local government had provided a few town residencies, but most live in the camp, two to a room. They share toilets and showers and eat in the cafeteria.

"Our land is planted mainly in bananas and guayaba," Enrique told me. "Banana workers receive a monthly advance of 500 pesos and the others 800. There is more work and profits in guayaba. We distribute profit-shares once a year. Some earn as much as 20,000 pesos over the advance.

"In this way, we have almost no departures within the year. After a couple years or so, some easterners take their savings and return to their birth place to build a house."

A national joke has it that Havanans, nicknamed *aseres*, accuse *naquitos*, those from Santiago de Cuba, of rejecting their home province for the preferred, more sophisticated Havana. *Naquitos* reply that they migrate, in order to save the homeland because so many *aseres* abandon Cuba for Miami and those who remain refuse to work hard.

Luis rose to leadership from the ranks as is common these days. Other farm leaders—heads of production and personnel—usually move up the ladder. No one is voted into power nor do the workers make most decisions, but they seem to have more desire to make suggestions.

"Regional leadership lets us pick our leaders. Few leaders come from the outside", Luis said.

"The idea of total worker control is a dream, which most workers are not prepared for."

It seems that Luis is more popular and respected by the workers than is the case with Matías. But both share work discipline philosophy.

"Leadership must discipline workers, in order to prevent our passionate temperaments from taking control," Luis said.

Edgardo and Guillermina agreed.

"Most naquitos and other easterners are not self-disciplined and don't easily settle in as usufructuaries of the land. So, yes, leadership must demonstrate discipline, but there are ways and ways of doing this."

Salt of the Earth

Alejandro stood on top of a pile of shit—animal dung used for fertilizer. A score of workers watched him jump up and down on it, apparently in an effort to loosen it all.

"Quite appropriate place for you, my mate. You are always in the shit," I called out from my bicycle.

For once Alejandro didn't know how to reply. He just laughed. One of the onlookers quipped:

"Ron won the jodedor (joker) post for the day."

I was heading back to Havana and from there to my home in Denmark. We were saying farewell for now á la Cubana.

The night before, Guillermina had bought and prepared another chicken for our last dinner while Edgardo told me about his time in an international mission.

Edgardo and Guillermina, both naquitos, met at a school where he worked as a mechanic and she as a cook. Edgardo was also in the army reserves. Angola's progressive government was then under armed attack by the apartheid South African government, which supported the right-wing counter-revolutionaries.

Angola asked Cuba for assistance and it complied, sending many thousands of volunteer soldiers.

In the 1960s, 70s and 80s, Cubans assisted many governments in defending their countries under attack by US-friendly, repressive governments. This was the case with Angola, Ethiopia, Nicaragua and a few secret missions elsewhere.

CIA propaganda claimed that President Fidel Castro forced Cubans to fight and die on foreign shores.

"That is one more of their many lies," Edgardo told me.

"I volunteered for an international mission, in 1983, when the army called for volunteers. We received medical check-ups and training in combat. We were not told where we would be sent but we had two opportunities to back out. First when called upon and then at the airport before departure.

"When we received word that we were to fight in Angola and that this was the last chance to accept the international solidarity mission or not, five or six men out of my company of 160 decided to stay in Cuba. There was no problem for them. They simply returned to their jobs or stayed in the army at home."

Edgardo recounted the harsh conditions everyone lived under during his 28 months in Angola. There was often no where to sleep but on the ground or in hammocks. They sometimes had to hunt their food. Many native and Cuban soldiers fell sick or died of diseases; many died from wounds.

Although he fought many battles, Edgardo was not wounded. He was promoted to first sergeant and headed a squadron of men.

"I confronted many horrible sights, of which I care not to speak. Like so many others, I volunteered to fight, because our country has an ethic of brotherhood. Most Cubans were originally Africans forced into slavery. Our revolution did away with racist discrimination, slavery's successor.

"But our brothers and sisters in Africa are still subjugated to racist oppression and thievery of their resources by dominating foreign governments, such as was the case in Angola in those years. I could not sit by and do nothing."

When Edgardo returned home, he resumed his job at the school and his love relationship with Guillermina. They soon wed. After their children, by earlier partners, had grown and left home, they decided, in 1993, to volunteer for the farm contingent then working the land where they are now.

After a tasty dinner, we three watched, alongside several neighbors, Santiago de Cuba's baseball team win the series against Havana's Industrial team.

In the morning, we ate a filling breakfast and Guillermina prepared me a sandwich for the road. Our embraces lingered. Then Edgardo told me: "Nothing will break our friendship. We are your family here. You come whenever you can. You are not a foreigner but our brother, one more Cuban completing an international mission."

Chapter Twelve: Health for All

When I lived in Cuba during its hardest economic years, Cuba's budgetary expenditures remained oriented to human welfare for all. No one went without free medical care and education. No school or clinic was closed down. Yet more people did get sick for lack of proper nutrition.

I was hit by bronchitis and had to take penicillin injections. My family doctor gave me the medicine so that I could give a dosage to any doctor or nurse anywhere in Cuba so they could inject me. One day I was far from my local clinic and went into the nearest hospital. Within 15 minutes and with no paperwork or questions asked I was injected.

The last time it was necessary for me to be in the United States, my ears became stuffed with wax. I had no family doctor so I went to a clinic. After two hours wait, a doctor looked into my ears. He said there was no sickness so he would not remove the deafening wax. He said I must go to my own doctor. He wanted $200 for his five minutes and no treatment. I ran out of the clinic without paying.

One key indicator showing both Cuba's growth in this decade and the moral and politically humane will of the government is the increase in state expenditures in the area of human rights. This will was codified in the 1976 constitution.

"The state...guarantees that no sick person be left without medical care."

Today, the world's "greatest democracy" lags behind its small "scoundrel" rival in the Caribbean in providing health care and education for its people. One barometer, infant mortality—which the World Health Organization considers as a "thermometer of social well-being"—shows Cuba with 5.6 deaths per 1,000 live births compared to the US, where in 2005 it stood at an average of 6.5, but there were 14.5 deaths for black babies.

In Cuba, there is no color distinction between health conditions and health care.

The United Nations Development Program (UNDP) has devised universal indicators for human development and equity in which the three main aspects are: a long and healthy life, acquisition of knowledge and a decent standard of living.

A study published in the December 2005 Medicc Review shows Cuba at the top of all Latin American countries in providing the greatest opportunities for human expansion and the elimination of unnecessary and avoidable inequalities considered unjust.

This study is based on statistics and reports by UNDP, WHO, FAO and related regional organizations looking at: longevity, literacy rate, access to safe drinking water, student-teacher ratio, physicians per inhabitants, environmental protection, even television sets per inhabitants.

"The combination of free and universal health care and education, public participation, and the willingness by the government to implement policies to maximize equity, has had positive effects on health outcomes," wrote Medicc Review.

In September 2000, all heads of state of all 189 United Nation-member countries agreed to measure progress towards eliminating extreme poverty by 2015. They established eight goals—known as MDG for Millennium Development Goals—with 18 targets.

Four years later, Cuba submitted a report on its developments. Some goals have already been met: universal primary education; gender equality and empowerment; reduction of child mortality.

Cuba's judgment was that it was on track within the deadline on the remaining goals. Maternal mortality rate, for example, had fallen from 57 per 100,000 births to 38.5, in the last decade. Almost all Cubans (95.2%) had access to potable water and plumbing (94.2%).

Other indicators at the start of last year were: under five mortality rate: 7.7 per 1000, which was better than the average of the "most developed" countries (10) and lowest of "developing" countries (89-161); 99% of births attended by professional staff; 5.5% of low-birth weight babies.

Cuba has one of the fastest ageing populations: 15.4% are over 60 years old. Instead of cutting back on old aged benefits, as is done by capitalist governments, they are increased. In 2005, the minimum pension was raised by 50%.

Other comparisons between socialist Cuba and capitalist United States and the United Kingdom showed remarkable human rights advantages that socialism provides its people in contrast to private profiteering economies.

The following facts and figures are taken from each government's budgets and relative ministries, from WHO, UN Millennium Development Goals, CIA Factbook, Cuban Economic Studies Centre, Cuban Armed Forces Review 1997, January 2002 NACLA, Cuba's "Granma", and the US magazine "Medicc Review".

It must be noted that officially Cuba values its peso on a 1-1 scale with the US. In 1994, however, the real value was 150 to $1. In 2006, the peso was valued at 24 to one dollar.

	1994	2005	2006
Budget expenses	14.5bn	22bn	25.7bn
Education	9.2%	19%	19.4%
Health	7.4%	12%	12.5%
Defence/police	4.7%	6.7%	7%
Social security	10.5%	15%	13.6%
Housing/municipal	2.5%	6%	5.5%

The United States budget for 2006 was $2.8 trillion dollars, of which $64.5 billion (2.3%) went to education. Officially, the country used $558 billion (20%) for "defense" and current wars. But at least 17% more of its budget in hidden expenses went to pay for former wars: for veteran injuries and benefits, and for its national war debt.

The two distinctive economic systems expend their state budgets based upon different values—the one emphasizing collective well-being and each person's need for good health and education, the other on private property and individual welfare for the wealthy.

The United States and the UK accuse Cuba of being a systematic abuser of "human rights": yet the US spends much more money on wars than on human welfare, while Cuba does the opposite. Here are some results for 2004-5.

	Cuba	USA	UK
Life expectancy	77	77	78.5
Infant mortality	5.6	6.5	5.1
Doctors per pop	1–161	1–280	
HIV	0.1%	0.6%	
Literacy	100%	97%	99%
Unemployment	1.9%	5%	4.7%
Poverty	0	12%	17%

In Cuba, there is no difference in salaries for gender or race while there are large differences in the US and UK. Real poverty and illiteracy are non-existent in Cuba while 40% of Latin Americans live in poverty, 42 million people (9%) are illiterate, and 1 in 10 are unemployed.

No one goes homeless or starves as is the case for many millions in both the US and UK.

Cuba has the lowest infant mortality rate of all Latin American and developing countries. All children are vaccinated against 13 diseases free of charge, and Cuba produces 12 of these vaccines.

Havana's extensive scientific centre includes some of the most advanced biotechnology research and production laboratories in the world. The Center for Genetic Engineering and Biotechnology (CIGB), for example, has a new recombinant human growth factor product, Citoprot-B—an injection treatment for diabetic ulcers—which is the only alternative to the otherwise necessary amputation of limbs.

Citoprot-B has proven to be 85-90% effective. This will prevent many of Cuba's 3000 people from losing their limbs in annual amputation, because half of them are caused by diabetic foot.

On the other hand, the US Centers for Disease Control and Prevention reports that one-third of children born in the US in 2000 will develop diabetes. That horrible reality will affect between 45 and 50 million people by mid-century.

Thanks to the US blockade against Cuba, their own people do not benefit from Cuba's cures against several diseases. This is currently the case, for example, for those affected by Hepatitis B and Meningitis B for which Cuba has effective vaccines. There was no case of the former disease in the past five years.

Although Cuba originated the only cure against Meningitis B, children continue to die in the US because it will not import the vaccine.

Chapter Thirteen: Education for All

It was popular in the 1960s-70s for back-packing hippies and professional musicians to travel to India in search of spiritual values and experiences. Many of these and other well-meaning First World people wishing to help illiterate, out-of-school children pay a monthly sum to sponsor a child's education.

Although the state runs primary schools without direct costs to families, millions of families simply have no money for school materials or clothing and must use their children to work for a living.

Though there has been progress in decreasing the numbers of poor and illiterates, India still has the world's greatest numbers of illiterates, 350 million, and out-of-school children.

A 2001 UNICEF report showed that 20% of children from ages six to fourteen did not attend school, and women were still predominately illiterate. UNICEF pointed to the causes: inadequate instructions and poorly educated teachers, the caste and class system, discrimination of women, forced child labor, and a general system based on unequal opportunities.

The Indian government, apparently, would rather accept that one-fourth of its people are impoverished and 35% are illiterate than they would choose an economic system and government that would guarantee:

"That no child be left without schooling, food and clothing; that no young person be left without opportunity to study; that no one be left without access to studies, culture and sports."

Such a commitment is the choice of the Cuban people and their government, as codified in their socialist constitution.

Within a couple years following the 1959 revolution, 100,000 voluntary education *brigadistas* taught 707,000 to read and write, thus eliminating illiteracy. Under Batista, there was 23% illiteracy and 44% of primary school-aged children did not attend school. Only 17% of secondary school-aged children attended school. By 1961, the revolutionary government had secured each child a classroom. The 10,000 unemployed teachers under Batista, one-quarter the entire number, were all teaching with a raise in pay. The educational budget had been tripled. Ten thousand new classrooms had been constructed and were in use.

Not one Cuban child, even in the hardest economic years, has gone without schooling nor have his parents paid one cent—not even taxes—for the nation's extensive educational system.

Cuba is not richer than India or most of the many other countries where illiteracy and out-of-school children abound. The significant difference—which guarantees all Cubans free education plus free health care, cultural and sports activities, necessary food on the table, and roof over head—is the Cuban decision to collectivize the economy and thus share the wealth they all produce. And their ideological slogan plays a stimulating role: "Every worker a student and every student a worker."

The leaders of most nations decided in Dakar five years ago to assure universal primary education by 2015, yet most state leaders do nothing or all too little to keep their promise. Cuba and Venezuela do.

In 2004, these nation's leaders—Fidel Castro and Hugo Chavez—signed an agreement to ensure that goal not only for Venezuela but for all Latin Americans.

"Dawn" is the treaty's name, or ALBA in Spanish, the Bolivarian Alternative for Latin America. This pact is based on mutual cooperation, solidarity and respect and is their answer to United States capitalism's ALCA plan for both American continents. ALCA—like the current NAFTA agreement between the US, Canada and Mexico—favors unrestricted marketing, neo-liberalism, so that transnational companies and the US could dominate even more than they do now.

Mexico, for example, went from being a corn exporter before NAFTA to being an importer with additional unemployment for six million former corn farmers.

Castro and Chavez, and now Bolivia's President Evo Morales, seek to create programs that can bring food to all stomachs and for thought. ALBA removes trade barriers and customs taxes—not just for the rich—and provides investments for all member nations by increasing intra-regional bank cooperation.

Under these 2005-6 provisions, Venezuela was financing some Cuban industrial and road construction projects, and it was selling 90,000 tons of oil daily to Cuba at $27 per ton instead of the world price of $75.

A key provision of ALBA is to bring literacy, further education, and health care to the entire continent south of the United States-NAFTA border. Cuba is providing 13,000 doctors and nurses, 70% of all public health personnel, to Venezuela, and a comparable number of medical personnel to other Latin American and Africa nations.

The first part of the educational goal, alphabetization of all Venezuelans, was rapidly achieved. The program, known as Mission Robinson, is financed by Venezuela and manned by thousands of Cuban teachers. In less than two years, they have taught 1.5 million Venezuelans to read and write.

Educational missionaries set up courses so that 162,000 Venezuelan youths, who otherwise could not have attended high school, had been able to study and achieve secondary school diplomas by early 2006.

Mission Robinson uses the Cuban study technique—"Yes I Can"—in twenty countries in Latin America, Africa and even to natives in New Zealand.

ALBA also bolsters Cuba's revolutionary tradition of offering free university education, especially medical training, to the poor from the Third World. Fashioned after Cuba's Latin American Medical School (ELAM), built in 1998, a second ELAM is being built in Venezuela. It will be the tenth medical school in Latin America and Africa founded by Cuba professors since 1976 when the first one was built in Yemen.

Venezuela's ELAM will be able to provide free medical training for 100,000 physicians over a decade. This commitment will amount to the equivalent of a $20-30 billion contribution to developing countries.

The first 1,500 medical students from 28 countries graduated from Cuba's ELAM in July 2005. Another 100 graduates had studied in different MD programs, which Cuba has had for four decades. In all, 4,000 international medical students have been graduated. A similar number of international students have also graduated in other fields.

Cuba even accepts poor students from the United States, where Third World conditions exist for many millions. There were 88 US American graduates at the first ELAM ceremony: 85% were not white and 73% were female.

ELAM's commitment is to enroll at least 2,000 youths annually. Not only is the six-year medical education free of charge, but so is accommodations and food, and equipment. All they need do is agree to return to their countries and practice medicine in the interests of the patients, especially the poor. In the case of the US students, this is a tall order.

Forty-five million Usamericans have no heath care coverage. And although a medical education costs around $300,000, the US blockade forbids students to study in Cuba, albeit free of charge—or, should I say, precisely because it is free education. US residents who study in Cuba risk fines of $200,000, and up to ten years in prison—just for studying, in order to help the poor.

Part of Cuba's educational program is oriented to achieving full social justice with equality for its own people. Since the beginning of this century, the government has been conducting a campaign known as "Battle of Ideas".

The campaign is based on Cuba's liberation hero José Martí's ideal that "no social justice is possible without educational equality". Che Guevara interpreted Martí's ideal by considering the whole of Cuba as one great university.

The "Battle of Ideas" aims to promote and reinforce solidarity consciousness, especially in light of the far-reaching techniques used by cultural imperialism to counteract solidarity with individualism. It begins in day care centers with the "Educate your child" program using non-formal ways of training, including the use of television programs..

In 2006, Cuba had five television stations instead of two a decade ago. Two of these channels are educationally oriented. Teachers use these channels video programs. Children also learn computer skills in primary school. English is taught from the third grade onward.

Primary classes were down to a student-teacher ratio of 1 to 20, and even a lower ratio for 428 schools for children with disabilities. Classrooms had been organized in hospitals and in children's homes taught by peripatetic teachers.

Pre-university education had been expanded and the student-teacher ratio reduced to 1-30.

All teachers are trained to become educators responsible for the all-round education of a set number of students.

A new group of peripatetic teachers, the José Martí Contingent, included 4,000 art instructors teaching visual arts, music, theater and dance in all communities.

Another program, "study as work", provided three hours of classes four days a week and part-time jobs to 150,000 young people, who had neither studied nor worked.

Fifty thousand new teachers, who would otherwise not have become teachers, had been graduated through these work-study courses in the past three years. Cuba has the most teachers per capital in the world: one to every 37 inhabitants.

Another 20,000 secondary school graduates had been trained as social workers while pursuing a university education. These "doctors with souls" deal with human problems. They frequent homes where families have special needs, such as: elderly people, those with disabilities and social behavior problems.

The "Battle of Ideas" also seeks to universalize higher education. The universalization of higher education was assured, in 2006, by doubling state educational expenditures—one-fifth the national budget.

The Minister of Education, Juan Vela Valdes, reported, in July 19, 2006, that Cuba's network of university classes was functioning in 3,150 localities covering all the country's 169 municipalities.

Four hundred thousand people were studying at university level in this way. Many take courses part-time while working. Another 86,000 students were studying full-time at Cuba's 65 universities. These one-half million people studying at a university level represented 4.5% of the population. At the time of the revolutionary victory, Cuba had only three state universities and one private. Total enrolment was 20,000.

Since the revolutionary victory, Cuba has graduated 800,000 university students of a population of 11.2 million people.

Former Minister of Education, Dr. Luis Gómez Gutiérrez, explained Cuba's Battle of Ideas to participants of the World Conference on Basic Literacy Training held in Havana, February 2005, in this way:

"The idea is to reach everybody, that no one is ever abandoned or unattended. Education reaches everyone from early childhood and throughout life...excluding no one. We pin our hopes on this utopia and the results we have obtained breathe life into our optimism. We are building the fairest, most equal society that has ever been known to the history of humankind."

Chapter Fourteen: Exporting Human Capital

Cuba's constitution is based on "proletarian internationalism, on the fraternal friendship, aid, cooperation and solidarity of the peoples of the world."

In the nation's 2004 report to the United Nation's Millennium Development Goals, adopted in 2000 by 189 heads of state, it demonstrated that is had met three of the eight humanitarian goals designed towards eliminating extreme poverty by 2015, and that it was on track with the rest. Cuba's foreign policy is, in fact, based upon the eighth goal: "Develop a global partnership for development".

As of 2006, twenty-five thousand of the nation's 70,000 doctors and several thousand other medical personnel are serving in 68 countries; a similar number of teachers and technicians serve in a total of 100 countries.

Cuba is building a medical university in Venezuela. Over the last three decades, it has built others in: Equatorial Guinea, Ethiopia, Uganda, Ghana, Gambia, Yemen, Guinea Bissau Guyana and Haiti.

In addition to providing health care and education, Cuban collaborators assist 24 of the most underdeveloped nations with other technical advice, aid to HIV victims, and sugar.

In June 2001, the UN General Assembly met to discuss Aids. Cuba offered "doctors, teachers, psychologists, and other specialists needed to assess and collaborate with the campaigns to prevent Aids and other illnesses; diagnostic equipment and kits necessary for the basic prevention programmes and retrovirus treatment for 30,000 patients...Cuba will not charge and will pay the salaries in its national currency."

Under pressure from the US, the offer was rejected—"Democracy" over health being the determining factor. But eight African and six Latin American countries accepted Cuba's Aids intervention project, offering education programs and treatment of 200,000 patients, and the training of half a million health workers.

The export of "human capital", as the state characterizes these missions, is provided to individual recipients free of charge. In most cases, the states, which receive Cuba's aid, pay in some form, such as by bartering oil, other resources and manufactured products.

Cuba's commitment to serving the poor, the sick and victims of natural catastrophes is a glaring contrast to the conduct of world capitalism led by the United States and particularly its current government.

A good example of this is how the governments confronted the damage caused in August 2005 by Hurricane Katrina in New Orleans and Mississippi and Alabama. Cuba immediately offered to help save survivors with the specially formed Henry Reeves International Team of Medical Specialists in Disasters & Epidemics.

Fifteen hundred medical professionals committed themselves to assist Katrina's victims. Each was equipped with 50 pounds of medicines—a total of 36 tons of medical supplies—and field hospital equipment. These missionaries had an average of ten years clinical experience and had served in 43 countries. The Bush regime did not even have the decency to reply to the humanitarian offer. Instead it "absorbed the loss" of 1,800 people, who died simply for lack of aid and treatment.

The Henry Reeves teams were sent instead to aid Pakistani earthquake victims and Guatemalans affected by Hurricanes Stan and Wilma.

Most of the 2,500 doctors and paramedics served half-a-year in Pakistan. By April 2006, they had treated 1.5 million patients—73% of patients hit by the disaster—performed 13,000 surgical operations, trained 660 Pakistani medics and turned over the 32 field hospitals they brought with them. The Cuban government also donated 241 tons of medicines and surgical instruments, and 275 tons of hospital equipment.

The Cubans were most noted for taking on the toughest assignments, climbing mountainous areas and working with the poorest of the poor who had never been visited by a doctor.

Dictator Pervez Musharraf, a close ally and friend of Bush, officially thanked Cuba and acknowledged that it had sent more disaster aid than any other country, including the United States.

In 2006, Henry Reeves volunteers numbered 3,000. They are required to speak at least two languages and be competent in epidemiology.

This mission's namesake was taken from the United States Civil War veteran who served in Cuba's first war of independence from Spain. Reeves, a New Yorker, earned the rank of brigadier general. He died in battle, in 1876, after having fought in 400 battles.

"Recognition of Cuban expertise in disaster preparedness and response" promoted the UN Development Program and Association of Caribbean States to select Havana as headquarters for the new Cross Cultural Network for Disaster Risk Reduction, which is to facilitate regional cooperation in disaster management, wrote MEDICC Review, summer 2005.

In 2004, Cuban doctors began applying what their associate scientists had created, a simple surgery which cures many forms of blindness within two to three days. By mid-2006, a quarter million people, in 24 countries, had been cured of cataracts, retractile disorders, corneal glaucoma, myopias and strabismus. Cuba had 14,000 doctors working in poor areas, and many conservative Venezuelan doctors complained of the free competition but refused to offer them aid. 100,000 Venezuelans regained their eyesight in the first year of Cuba's Operation Miracle program.

Fidel Castro and Venezuela's President Hugo Chavez had agreed to provide funds, medicines and medical personnel to treat those suffering from these eye afflictions, which are frequently caused by mal-nutrition. Over one million Latin Americans are affected annually, and the two nations plan to operate on that many each year over a decade.

Cuban medical missionaries carrying backpacks with hospital equipment and medicines reach into the far corners of Latin America to perform the surgeries.

"The world has never witnessed anything equal to this health program," commented San Vicente-Granadian Prime Minister Ralph Gonsalves upon landing in Havana last February.

The state leader came to thank Cuba for having cured 1000 blind citizens in yet another foreign aid program, Operation Miracle.

In the case of San Vicente-Granada, only a few personnel could arrive at a time in small aircraft since there is no international airport for larger craft. So, Cuba and Venezuela, agreed to build one through their ALBA cooperative trade pact.

Tens of thousands of blind patients not treated where they live were being transported to Havana for the surgeries. This program is also paid for through ALBA. The largest numbers came from Venezuela but they also came from the entire continent and the Caribbean. Poor blind people in the United States may apply as well.

Many patients were spending a short recovery in spacious top floor rooms of the tall apartment building, Focsa, where I had lived for four years. Thousands more were occupying hotel rooms previously used by the tourist industry. As many as 1,650 patients received eye operations at 20 hospitals in one single day, on August 20, 2005.

Mission Robinson was educating hundreds of thousands of illiterates and out-of-school children in a score of Third World Countries and New Zealand natives.

Besides providing literacy and further education, Cuba also provides cultural and sports programs. Artists and coaches impart their knowledge and skills across the globe. It sometimes occurs that a sport teams trained by Cubans compete with Cuban teams. The coaches often feel double loyalties when it comes to which team they wish to win.

In addition to the free solidarity aid Cuba provides to millions of people in their own countries, it also offers free higher education, emphasizing medical training, to hundreds of thousands more at Cuban schools. International enrolment in Cuban medical classes were more than doubled from 2004-5 to 2005-6 classes. Thirty thousand students from 30 countries were then studying to become doctors, nurses, dentists, allied health personnel and health psychologists.

Since the beginning of Cuba's revolution, its foreign policy has been oriented to assist all Third World nations, especially Latin Americans, Caribbeans and Africans to tear themselves away from foreign domination, which keeps their peoples in poverty, ignorance and ill health. The strong voice of President Fidel Castro has been a beacon to many of these nations, which recently have been taking heed.

Between 1963 and 2005, more than 100,000 doctors and health care workers had helped people in 97 countries. In 2005, the 25,000 health professionals helped the most deprived areas in 26 countries of Africa and Latin America. They delivered over one million babies, administered 9 million vaccinations, and conducted 1,657,867 operations.

Cuba provides more medical humanitarian aid than all the United Nations countries, through World Health Organization, deploys. No other nation in the world, nor private body or international organization, has made such a commitment to a universal medical program—not in general nor in any specific area, such as Cuba's Operation Miracle.

The progressive, new leaders of Argentina, Brazil and Uruguay, along with Paraguay, have formed the regional trade organization Mercosur, whose agenda is similar to that of the more progressive ALBA—Venezuela, Cuba and Bolivia. Mercosur adopted 32 projects, at the end of 2005, amounting to $4 billions to be completed in the next five years. In 2006, Mercosur accepted Venezuela as a member.

It is noteworthy that Paraguay joined despite strong protest from the United States, which is seeking to impose its imperial trade plan, ALCA, over both American continents. Paraguay's government has otherwise been quite compliant in allowing the US to build military bases aimed at threatening progressive Latin American governments and the people's guerrilla movements in Colombia.

Yet another regional trade plan, CAN, covers the Andes area. Members are: Bolivia, Chile, Ecuador, Guyana, Peru, Surinam, Venezuela, and even Colombia.

It is the hope of most Latin American leaders and people that Mercosur, CAN and ALBA will eventually lead to the formation of the United States of South America, bringing an end to United States imperialism in its "backyard".

Irene Zamalea (seated, centre) was the first woman neurosurgeon in Cuba — and in Latin America. Seen here at a meeting in Santa Clara, Cuba, in 2003

Chapter Fifteen:
Media Openings

"Citizens have freedom of speech and of the press in keeping with the objectives of socialist society." This is the law, according to Cuba's 1976 constitution as last amended in 2002.

In Fidel Castro's famous "words to intellectuals", June 30, 1961, the state leader stated what the constitution later codified in law: "...the revolutionary places something even above his own creative spirit; he places the Revolution above all else, and the most revolutionary artist would be disposed to sacrifice even his own artistic vocation for the Revolution... Writers and artists who are not revolutionary must have the opportunity and liberty to express themselves within the Revolution. This means that within the Revolution [it is] everything; against the Revolution—nothing..."

When, in 1999, UPEC (the Journalists Union of Cuba) promoted the flourishing of digital journalism, Castro spoke about journalists' role: "A journalist has to be a statesman, because he's defending the identity and culture."

When I worked in Cuba for Editorial José Martí and Prensa Latina (1987-96), the media was tightly controlled by the Communist party political bureau. I know from first hand experience that the concept of journalist as "statesman", as revolutionary first, meant that many ideas or attempts to write about many economic or political aspects of society, or to dig into corruption by persons in key positions or to question government or Communist party policy was absolutely taboo.

The line between "everything" within the revolution and "nothing" against the revolution was never clear. Most journalists never tried to employ investigative journalism or to write anything that might be taken critically by media directors or by the party propaganda organ.

In 1994, a few changes occurred. Some of the media began to criticize inefficiency, indolence and thievery. But critique stopped at the rank-in-file and never delved into any systematic pattern or into possible policy errors.

Any observer of world politics knows that the unfriendly neighbor to the north makes every effort to manipulate the world mass media and to subvert Cuba. I know from personal experiences as a reporter and editor in the United States in the 1960s-70s. No lie, no undermining tactic is excluded. "Black propaganda" the CIA calls it. Bush's government even has a bureau whose brazen purpose is to control the world mass media, fabricating lies in defense of "freedom and democracy".

Many authors have documented how the US consistently uses the media to overthrow governments it does not like, and some have been written by their own agents [1].

It is a fine art to discover a satisfying formula of how to balance society's need for critical expression and the need to defend a worthy social-economic system. In the April 18, 2006 Rebelión.org interview with Ricardo Alarcón, Cuba's parliamentary president, he recognized the dilemma: "It's true that there's a kind of `self-censorship´ pretty much addressed in our media. It has to do with a style, a way of working, that's just one of the negative remnants of the Soviet model."

I feel these introductory remarks are necessary in order to place the Cuban media into its concrete historical and political perspective. Freedom of expression, of the press is never limitless.

Cuba media is reforming today. It still does not criticize top leadership but it delves deeper into what goes wrong in major areas of the economy, into services provided by the state, into social corruption and weak revolutionary moral among some Cubans. Taboos are being broken.

This indicates that leadership feels that there is such a need and that they and the people can cope with criticism.

In the first months of 2006 I read several investigative and critical articles in the major daily press. I cite two examples from "Granma", the party daily. The February 16 issue featured a two-page spread, "The old dilemma of trash", in which three reporters interviewed officials responsible for garbage and rubbish collection.

Sanitary workers must pick up rotten food and all sorts of rubbish with bare hands as there are few gloves and shovels. And while part of the social system methodically eliminates conditions that breed malaria-carrying mosquitoes, the departments dealing with trash collection offer excellent conditions for all sorts of vermin.

This dilemma causes poor hygiene, exacerbated by disorderly garbage collection, scarcity of containers, parts and tools, and the lack of social consciousness by many unscrupulous persons who profit from the chaos, such as the "divers" who spread garbage from containers in order to find refuse that can be recycled and sold, and thieves who steal parts of or entire containers.

This situation provides fodder for the "new rich" against which the state is waging a morality propaganda campaign. The tremendous shortage of collection materials encourages private vehicle owners to charge people in some districts to haul away rubbish laying on streets and sidewalks. In addition to fees collected, these parasitical entrepreneurs plunge through the trash to find things that can be recycled and sold.

"Granma" concluded that authorities must take "major action" to correct this "disorder" which produces poor hygiene.

In the same month, "Granma" ran a series on why distribution of food is inefficient, why so many irregularities and discrepancies exist in the farmer markets, and why some people get rich as intermediaries. "Granma" interviewed top leaders in the industry, some of whom are also members of the Council of State. Some of them disagreed with each other over the causes of the problems and their cures.

The bureaucracy was criticized for being top heavy. For example, 40% of the 17,000 employees of the state distribution system (Acopios) are "administrators and bureaucrats".

The handful of national newspapers and most of the provincial papers now have columns which deal with reader complaints, mostly service-related problems, in which government organisms fail to resolve a problem. Some columns tackle thievery, such as post office employees who steal mail or open packages if they believe they may contain something of value.

While there now are letters-to-the-editor and a few debate articles, they are limited mainly to complaints about services. There are no critical commentaries of inadequacies of Communist party policy or of the state controlled socio-economic-political system, nor suggestions for changes of policy from the public.

Television has improved its programming of world news, analysis and documentaries about important world issues. Now that there are five national television stations, the country has a total of 58 television stations. One person in 3.5—the equivalent of one per family—owns a TV set.

The educational programs are excellent tools for schools, for youth and adults, and they present many international documentaries on nature, threats to the environment, the terror wars and laws. Telesur, the new Venezuela-sponsored Latin America answer to CNN, is also a daily ration.

Practically every family owns at least one radio; four million are in use. They listen to one or more of 225 radio stations, many of which have complaint programs.

Cuba had 1,700 websites by late 2005, according to Cubasi, which has one of them. Less than a year later, the country maintained 2900 websites. Newspapers, magazines, radio stations, television channels and audiovisual media had established 808 websites by mid-2006. They contain forums on diverse socio-political and cultural topics. Twenty Cuban media organizations publish in English. Journalists themselves have more than 200 personal web pages or weblogs, as do other professionals.

Other major categories with websites includes: the arts and humanities (682); medicine-technology and science (227); economy and business (122); education (90); societies, clubs and associations (71); internet and computing (60).

The list is longer and is kept up by Dana Lubow (danalubow.org/SPT).

Despite the growth of websites and blogs, Cuba still lags behind many nations in IT, but this is due mainly to the US blockade, which controls access to oceanic cabling and to internet. Cuba's government must pay exorbitant sums to a foreign company, in order to gain limited access with a narrow Internet band. Still, there are 150,000 internet users—mostly related to approved work centers—350,000 email users (many private persons), and between 200-300,000 personal computers. Nearly all schools have computers. (Figures are from early 2006.)

While there is progress in the quantity and type of information and analysis offered Cubans today, there are still taboo areas. If one tries to cross them, one still risks being considered a "dissident", or a counter-revolutionary serving the interests of US hegemonism, which is often the case. However, iconoclasm is allowed. "El cubano de la isla" (The Cuban from the Island) is one funky blogger, which some of the international media have cited.

If it weren't for the necessity of having convertible currency, there would be far more websites, bloggers and emails. Some control will be maintained, at least until the United States stops trying to overthrow the socialist economy and revolutionary government.

As the Commander-in-chief himself told the Federation of Latin American Journalists, November 12, 1999: "I understand very well how difficult it is to be a journalist in a socialist country...where the media and the press are not the private property of anyone...(but) the property of the people."

[1. See Philip Agee's "Inside the Company: CIA Diary", and my "Backfire: The CIA's Biggest Burn".]

Chapter Sixteen:
Cultural Rectification

The stout, broadly smiling chief editor ushered me into his small office. From the wall, the face of forbidden fruit—stern theoretician, military leader and organizer of the red army, "sorcerer" Leon Trotsky—stared defiantly down at me.

Editorial de Ciencias Sociales is one of Cuba's main book publishers. It had recently published a volume of the 1905 Russian revolution in which Trotsky's role is objectively portrayed. Since book publishing, and all media and cultural production, is overseen by the Communist party can one deduce that Cuba was going mad? Was the editor a treacherous Trot?

No, asserted the rather young editor, neither he nor the party was going Trotskyist or mad. It was real debate which the provocative intellectual wanted to accentuate.

Intellectuals have more leeway than ever before in terms of research, in discussing and publishing controversial ideas and analysis within leftist thought and practice than ever before. Editorial de Ciencias Sociales, for instance, publishes several books each year dealing with such ideas. None, however, challenge key decisions taken by the Cuban Communist Party or the state. Such challenges do not occur until these bodies conduct their own self-criticism.

I note two of Editorial de Ciencias Sociales books of the one hundred plus printed in 2005.

"Cuba sin dogma ni abandonos" (Cuba without dogma or abandonment). This collection of ten essays concerning the transition to socialism is written by Cuban professors. They reject specific models for constructing socialism-communism and tackle controversial Marxist themes: theory of the dictatorship of the proletariat, between perversion and historical necessity; rethinking the transition to a socialist economy; participatory democracy; revolutionary paternalism; and objectively describe Stalin, Trotsky and various left tendencies and praxis.

"Rusia del socialismo real al capitalismo real" (Russia from real socialism to real capitalism) provides a thoughtful academic analysis of Russian and Soviet Union developments. The two Cuban professors authors view the Soviet process primarily as a chronic of "political suicide", one which negatively influenced Cuba's own development but did not smother it.

Stalin and Stalinism are attacked for their brutality and for stifling critical thought, while Trotsky, Rosa Luxemburg, Gramsci and other Western Marxists are no longer dismissed as heretics.

In many respects, the current rethinking of Marxism and "real socialism" takes up from where Che Guevera left off in his early critique of Soviet economy and politics. In fact, this same publisher came out with the first publication of Che's critical notes of the Soviet economic model, in which he predicted its demise if the government did not change its bureaucratic, undemocratic and ineffective production and political methods.

Celia Hart, the physicist daughter of two of Cuba's top leaders: Haydeé Santamaria—one of the first two women guerrillas in the July 26 movement, who committed suicide in 1980—and Armando Hart—political bureau member and former minister of education and culture—is a prolific writer, who views Trotsky as having played a positive role in the revolutionary process.

Hart sees threads from Trotsky through much of the thinking of Che and Fidel. She asserts that Cuba is living up to Trotsky's concept of permanent revolution.

Fidel and other party leaders and intellectuals speak of the need to discard stifling models for socialism, which the Soviet Union imposed upon its allies. A breath of fresh air is blowing throughout society since the Special Period's first years of rugged adjustment to the fall of European state socialism.

The cultural institution, which Haydeé Santamaría founded, Casa de las Americas, sponsors seminars on Latin American culture and philosophical matters. I attended one on scientific socialism and utopia. Authors from several South American countries and Cuba discussed the need for Marxists and revolutionary socialists to dream, to place the subjective—the utopian—into the process of scientific socialism.

An Ecuadorian intellectual maintained that utopian ideas can be based upon reality. He said that multi-dimensional approaches are necessary to building socialism materially, and that there are no "laws of history", only processes.

Dreamers and realists converged at the gigantic annual book fair in Havana last February. Scores of seminars were held throughout the week. Dreamers were well received by large audiences for their visions of a future in which sensitive caring for one another would be modus operandi.

Twenty-seven Cuban publishers presented 520 new titles—all sold cheaply in national peso currency. Cuba has 188 book publishers in all. They printed 5.7 million copies of 520 new books and re-editions in 2005.

Seven-hundred thousand books were sold at the fair. This is a leap forward from the early-mid 1990s when book publishing was cut back to ten percent its previous production.

Venezuela was the fair's guest of honor. Its publishers brought five million copies of 1,200 titles. Half-a-million visitors had a chance to browse through Venezuela's and two score other foreign publishers' stalls, in addition to national publishing compartments.

Celia Hart's book, "Apuntes revolutionaries: Cuba, Venezuela y el socialismo internacional" ("Revolutionary notebooks") was to be found at the Spanish Foundación Federico Engels location.[3]

Her collection of essays and articles, many published first at rebelion. org, concentrates on the need for an ever-changing revolution, in order to succeed in shaping socialism and improving the material and subjective lives of all citizens. She sees hope in Cuba's future not only because of its internal growth but also because of the radical changes occurring regionally, especially in Venezuela and Bolivia.

While there were positive educational and entertaining books for all ages, cultural imperialism was allowed to creep in through some foreign publishers. A Mexican one, for instance, sold plastic Barbie dolls and folios about her.

I asked a family why they had bought one, and in precious convertible currency. "She is elegant, a good doll. Our children watch her on television and they wanted one," the mother replied. This family was, apparently, not attune to or in agreement with the "Battle of Ideas".

As the book fair traveled to 35 cities across the entire nation, many Cuban films were screened—a contrast to Usamerican glorifications of violence and consumerism.

Cannes winner "Viva Cuba" vividly presents daily problems and conflicts between parents who support the revolution and those who wish to migrate to Miami. Those who express dissatisfaction, who contend that "everything is illegal", are not condemned as evil. Even critique of some rituals performed by the young Pioneers, an objection to indoctrination, is shown.

The internationally renowned director-writer Humberto Salas' latest film, "Barrio Cubano", also portrays these themes, as well as thievery and corruption. I was not the only one in the theatre shedding tears at the conclusion.

In addition to the contradiction of making some of Hollywood's worst films available to Cubans there is the matter of what is not shown. Cuba and the world have listened to the joyous music of "Buena Vista Social Club". And tens of millions have seen the film of the now famous musicians, among them: Compay Segundo, Ibrahim Ferrer, Ruben González, Eliades Ochoa, whom Ry Cooder brought to us.

I dare say that this warm film has done more to promote Cuba—and, subtly, its fair social system—as a good place in this brutal world than any other single product or event. Yet when I asked Cuban musicians and others what they thought of it, they showed blank faces. No one had seen it! Why?

"We don't know why it wasn't shown here. But the media did write that the film existed and was well received world-wide," was the reply I received from all but one person, a sociologist.

He told me that a group of 20 sociologists "found" a video copy and viewed it as part of a sociological study. Asked if they would recommend that the state show it, he replied negatively.

"It is racist," he stated categorically, baffling me.

He recalled the scene where two black musicians are walking the streets of New York, admiring the city. His interpretation of this is that the film-maker wished to show "two monkeys coming out of the jungle and admiring 'civilization'".

I could only hope that this warped thinking was not behind the decision to not show the film.

Another example of unmentioned censorship is the Oliver Stone-made documentaries of Fidel Castro, "Comandante" and "Looking for Fidel". No one I spoke with had even heard of these films. Their existence was not made public. Why?

My speculation is that Fidel does not wish to reveal his private life, a bit of which reluctantly comes forth in "Comandante", and that he might think showing the film would be seen as presenting himself as a cult figure, something he and the state are most careful to avoid. Only dead heroes' images are widely portrayed before the population— an admirable aspect in promoting a popular, permanent revolution. "Looking for Fidel" concerns controversial issues: the few internal "counter-revolutionaries"; the death penalty, including for terrorists who kidnap people in hijackings as they attempt to flee for the "land of opportunities"; why Fidel does not step down as the leader and who will replace him. These matters are not openly discussed in the mass media, at least not by the public. Perhaps Fidel wants to keep it this way.

Chapter Seventeen: Revolutionary Morality

"This country can self-destruct; this Revolution can destroy itself, but they [the US] can never destroy us; we can destroy ourselves, and it would be our fault."

In his November 17, 2005 critical speech—on the 60th anniversary of his enrolment at the University of Havana—Fidel referred, for the first time publicly, to the ultimate consequence of a failed effort to develop a revolutionary consciousness among the population as a whole.

A disillusioned populace, one that pursues individual greed-consumerism, can destroy the Cuban revolutionary "project", something that the enemy cannot. That would mean that the key goal, which was Che's motto—"The ultimate and most important revolutionary aspiration: to see man liberated from alienation"—had not progressed sufficiently.

That the "maximum leader" made this reflection public is an enormous admission of the greatest actual challenge for this humanistic revolution. The ethical root to this dilemma—selfishness vs. holism—is, in fact, at the core of existence for the human race and the planet.

Progressive or revolutionary readers and supporters of Cuba must not shun our own reflection on this decisive question. A united, conscientious people can withstand the strongest enemy even when hungry—such as did the Vietnamese against China, France and the United States—but a morally disillusioned people cannot, not even with full stomachs.

Polarization or, as the bourgeois capitalists call it, democratic freedom, is based upon an appeal to individualism and coated with the surrendering supposition that mankind is born sinful, guilty, greedy, egoistic, and even evil.

The best that can be said about us is that we are born neutral and given a caring environment we can develop into a loving, and thus sharing and peaceful, race.

As an advocate of and sometimes participant in socialist revolution, I, alongside many Cubans, work for the human race's development into Che's "new man", or Jesus Christ's "love thy neighbor" human beings. We hope that not too many Cubans sink into the quagmire of individualism, into the "American Dream" of individualist opportunities for wealth.

This ideology is as powerful a weapon for capitalism-imperialism as is their police-military violence. It has captured the majority of working classes in most countries.

On the one hand, the Cuban people have braved the rigors of US imperialism. They have struggled up from the darkest days of the collapse of European state socialism, they have continued the egalitarian social network for all inhabitants and continue offering their "human capital" to poorer countries.

On the other hand, their lack of allies and the Special Period reforms have also caused large numbers of people to shun revolutionary morality, including but not exclusively the new rich sector.

As I was often told by several Cubans earlier this year, "We can't eat morality".

The Marxist intellectual Heinz Dietrich recently wrote about the unique survival of Cuba and revolutionary consciousness thusly: "During the long heroic phase of the Revolution, the overwhelming majority of the population fully identified with the process. But this identification is much more qualified today than in the heroic phase, for several reasons:

"Generational change, the fall of the USSR, the scientific and technological revolution, with its resulting processes of intensive accumulation and globalization, and the hampering affects of imperialist aggression on Cuba's endogenous economic and political development."

Leftist critics of those who openly express the existence of internal warts assert that such criticism is betrayal. They point to the vital need of shaping and maintaining unity—something that Cuban leaders have always stressed—in contrast to allowing its opposite—polarization—to divide people and thus allow the enemy to conquer them.

Yet, if we ignore the reality of disillusionment, we do nothing to avert its consequences. We should have learned this already, especially with the fall of state socialism, which was accomplished with hardly a whimper. In short, the working class had lost its revolutionary morality and turned its back on so-called socialism.

The Cuban revolution, for me, must succeed, not only for eleven million Cubans but as our beacon of hope for a better world. If Cuba "self-destructs", hundreds of millions will be lost in depression.

The world's monster realizes this. That is why it is so imperative for it to destroy the "bad example of the good example". And that is why we must confront our warts. As Dietrich asked, why else would Fidel feel the need to discuss the reversibility of the Revolution?

So, let's look at the problems!

When the Special Period in Times of Peace was launched in September 1990, and set fast with the July 26, 1993 "double-economy" declaration by a solemn Fidel, I was afraid that inequalities would lead not only to a new rich but to a class society. I began writing about this worry in some left media, but Prensa Latina, where I worked, would not publish such "subversive" thinking. Many foreign supporters of Cuba viewed me as a "traitor" for such expressions.

On November 24, 2005, Fidel Castro spoke on the popular round table TV program. For the first time publicly, he spoke of a "new class".

"We are well aware, that today there is a new class, in virtue of the phenomena [special period] that the Revolution has had to go through."

One of the possible future presidents, Minister of Foreign Affairs, Felipe Pérez Roque, followed suit in an address to the United Nations. He said that the danger for Cuba is the creation of a bourgeois class. Such a class can only come from small farmers and sections of the working class, who endeavor to get out of this class by hook or crook.

In the November 17 speech, Fidel asserted that the new rich would not win against socialism.

"I can assure you with absolute certainty that this battle against waste, theft, the illegal diverting of resources and other generalized vices has been won in advance…"

Fidel praised revolutionary efforts of the mass organizations and the new youth brigades—social workers—established to watch thievery by the working class and the petty bourgeoisie. Thousands of students, wearing blue t-shirts with white lettering that reads "social workers", have taken the place of workers at gas stations.

Fidel explained: "Certain vices can be very deep-seated. We started with Pinar del Rio to ascertain what was happening in the gas stations that sell gas in dollars. We soon discovered that there was as much gas being stolen as sold…in some places more than half."

"Well, what is happening in Havana? Will they mend their ways? Not really, everything is fun and games."

"In Havana Province, people learned to steal like crazy. Today, the social workers are in the refineries; they get on board the tanker trucks that carry 20,000 or 30,000 liters, and they watch, more or less, where that truck goes, and how much of the oil is rerouted. They have discovered private gas stations supplied with oil from these trucks."

French journalist-sociologist Danielle Bleitrach wrote an analysis of Fidel's important November 17 speech (see "Que pasa en Cuba", www.rebelion.org, May 18, 2006, and in English published by www.walterlippmann.com in his CubaNews@yahoogroups.com, July 3, 2006) in which she noted some of the results of the initiative Fidel assumed to combat epidemic corruption.

"The sweep is deep. A number gives a good idea: in 2005, the party rid itself of 2,900 members and several company directors and ministers were dismissed. In the workers assemblies, workers were invited to reflect on everything, to figure out the real cost of `inventar´ and the robberies. The consequences could be sanctions and expulsions but also jail sentences or transfers to sectors less `in play´. Some cases have been made public, but in general the measures have been taken discreetly in the work centers."

She defines Fidel's speech as being in "perfect synchrony with the Cuban mentality. The debate starts from a concrete fact, how to leave the Special Period, and ends with an investigation of socialism and the future of humanity. Right now it is centered in the concrete."

In Fidel's concrete (and idealistic) speech, he also referred to the fact that even before the Special Period systematic waste of the collective resources by most Cubans was ruining the economy. He said that it was "fortunate" that Cuba hadn't earlier discovered that there was a great deal of oil in their land and waters, "because it would have been wasted".

"Our nation is one of those that waste the most combustible energy in the world."

Much of this waste is not stolen but simply wasted by the citizenry's systematic neglect to turn off electricity (and water and gas) when not in use. Even the state is responsible, since an outdated switching network is incapable of shutting off street lamps during the light of day.

Besides the student guards against waste and thievery, the state has greatly increased the police force. Many people also have watch dogs, an indication that the people have enough food—that is not the problem.

Have Fidel and Pérez Roque become subversives or are they attempting to stop the growing negative reality in their nation? Is "the explication of Cuba", as Gabriel García Márquez has stated, that, "Fidel is both the head of government and the leader of the opposition". Or is the "opposition" also present among many Cubans, who truly advocate, and sometimes act for, a permanent revolution?

No doubt about it, history will certainly judge Fidel as the ultimate revolutionary strategist. And, quite the contrary to what the enemies of Cuba's socialist state claim, he is a gentle man, not apt to indulge in typical brutal purges that most of the world's leaders, given a chance, conduct. But he also has the backing of "a Cuban art to handle conflicts, to stop them: it is like an African word that means, `with a foundation of tenderness´", as Bleitrach so appropriately expressed.

I want to end this chapter with a long quote from the end of her essay.

"After having observed this first stage of the [self-criticism] process, one must admire the mastery with which it is being carried out, as much to achieve its primary objective, to improve the life of Cubans, as to the fact that there has been no excess, no blow of propaganda. The Cuban realism predominates and it does not try to divide: the `internal enemy´ is in everyone and everyone must examine their deficiencies collectively. There is in this much gentleness and a great knowledge of what it means to be human, with its qualities and defects, which are not fought with utopian tendencies, knowing full well that the fight is going to be hard.

"Cuba, as we have seen, is a society in arms, in an imposed war. An army has to feed and equip itself, but the subjective factor is fundamental to reaching victory. When the fight is for a whole continent, or for the whole planet, the people in the vanguard have a new mission: the one to oppose imperialism—still trying to destroy through `inventar´. The concrete goal and means to reach it are subjects of a permanent debate. In his speech, Fidel affirmed the concern that the Communists cannot resort to immoral means to reach a goal, and mentioned the German-Soviet pact as an example of that which Communists cannot do, because it is paid for with deep disrepute.

"One of the powers of the Cuban revolution, of its leaders and Fidel in particular, is this vindication of political ethics, shared by the population. To this war without limits, to the power of the Empire without apparent rival, only the resistance of the people can put it in check and perhaps destroy it. Cuba applies the strategy of Sun Tzu, to win the war without having to fight it."

Chapter Eighteen:
The Big Challenge;
forging communist consciousness

"Perhaps one of the most complicated dilemmas that the socialist revolution faces is how to achieve economic efficiency without renouncing the objective of creating a communist consciousness."

That is how Cuban central bank president Francisco Soberon Valdes described a central issue facing the country during his December 22, 2005 address to parliament.

"Certain actions committed during the special period, some imperviously necessary and others inexcusable errors, remove us from the strategic objective. The principal consequence of this situation has been greater levels of inequality and the waste of state resources."

Soberon asserted that corruption, fraud and theft are rampant and that "the majority of human beings are in the habit of not feeling satisfied with what they have and aspire to have more."

The "aspiration for more" is what capitalism's cynical ideologists count on to unrestrainedly sell their products, creating "needs" where they don't exist, making us sick from consumerism, which "minimizes the human spirit," he argued.

Immediate gratification is, perhaps, a universal craving, one which Buddhism's ascetic philosophy seeks to curb. Are we human beings, as a whole, capable of becoming communists?

This dilemma is not only Cuban but one that faces us all. But what is it that hinders the forging of communist consciousness in Cuba besides imperialism's omnipresent penetration?

"Greater production is necessary to overcome scarcity and the special period. But how to stimulate the workers?" asks University of Havana economist and state adviser Dr. Omar Everleny.

"They are more removed from the economy than in other economies, because most property and means of production are state-owned."

Does that mean that they do not identify with the state, with the collective ownership?

"You can't stimulate people with morality, with revolutionary propaganda, with anti-imperialism for a lifetime. People get tired of this and they must eat. Sure, everybody goes to the plaza for the marches, but, when they return home, they demand that the state provides them with their needs.

"That is why the state is now investing so much in economic improvements and in electricity savings."

My personal experiences back up Everleny's position. Many Cubans sell their rationed goods, purchased at below cost, to others for a profit. This waste of national resources is prompting the state to find a way to end the rationing of all goods, which has been a safety valve for the entire population since the beginning of the blockade in 1961.

Many Cubans rent and even sell their residences under the table for high sums. The state builds and sells all residences at cost. Most Cubans own their homes, but are not allowed to sell for profit. Speculation and profit-mongering are, after all, contrary to socialism.

Stealing whatever one can get one's hands on is so common that it is not considered theft, but simply "resolving a problem."

When I was in Havana, I noticed five men sitting under bushes in front of a ministry of education building. They explained that they were guarding a parked school bus donated by US group Pastors for Peace. The men were chauffeurs who drove ministry workers to and from work. When not driving, they guarded the bus.

One told me why this is necessary. "Nobody works hard in Cuba. We are either students, chiefs or guards. Production? Forget it. We must guard the bus because we are 11 million thieves." The others nod in agreement.

OK, they exaggerated, but they spoke what they felt. The fact that the state has employed many more policemen in recent times to watch out for criminal activities is proof of general concern.

Seven out of 10 times, when I paid for something with a convertible currency bill that more than covered the price, the employee did not return any change. When this was pointed out, the reply was always: "You are right. Excuse me," and the correct change was then delivered.

On two exceptional occasions, the worker followed me to return change when I had overpaid and walked away.

Then there are the innumerable people who refuse to see any moral infringement in wearing Yankee T-shirts bearing capitalist-imperialist slogans.

Some read: "I want to be a millionaire" next to a US dollar symbol, "I'm proud to be an American," "US army," "US marines," "US air force,"

"Someone went to Miami and all I got was this T-shirt" and, of course, the US flag.

Double-talkers will glibly say anything that they think you might want to hear, whether they believe so or not. They will also make promises and appointments with no intention of keeping them - part of the pre-socialist culture of "facilismo," an easy come, easy go attitude which the state, the political party and mass organizations have not managed to eradicate in half a century.

Perhaps the most controversial point that I could make involves state employees who render services to foreigners, either the more wealthy visitors to Cuba or poorer people in Third World countries.

The Historic Old Havana revitalization project employs black women to dress in colonial garb and walk about Spanish-style squares with large cigars between their red-painted lips. When I first saw this, I felt like puking.

Here are people liberated from colonialism, slavery and racist discrimination earning a living by portraying how it once was, but without any condemnation. They take "alms" from tourists who wish to photograph them. In fact, some of these women also offer their bodies for a price.

When I asked opinions about this of four acquaintances, only one shared my view. Three black friends said that they understood the "need" to perform. Again, it was for "survival."

But there are many other jobs these people could find or train for. No-one is starving in Cuba. No-one is forced to take on immoral tasks.

I end with the exporters of "human capital," as Fidel likes to call tens of thousands of fine Cubans who offer their education, hard work and caring for millions of people in scores of poor countries. They are the doctors, nurses, teachers, sports instructors and technicians working to save lives and improve the lives of millions.

How could I find fault with these good people? Certainly most truly want to be helpful, want to act in the solidarity spirit of revolutionary morality. Yet many also have a more selfish, albeit understandable motive. This aspect is one that I heard many Cubans complain about or speak of in envious terms.

"Resolving a problem" is the answer - that of buying home appliances or automobiles not realistically available for them on their Cuban peso wage at home. The price of a new automobile, for instance, would take a Cuban doctor or factory or field worker a lifetime to pay for.

Cuba sends abroad its best educated at no cost to the individual recipient, but the governments of these countries pay hard currency for the "volunteer" workers, who then purchase expensive items and transport them to Cuba or they buy such items at the "dollar shops" in Cuba.

This is not corrupt or "wrong," but this case of mixed motivations indicates that revolutionary morality is not so easily discerned.

Many of us left-wing Cuba supporters - especially those of us who are frustrated by living in the richest lands where we have not convinced our working classes to engage in overthrowing capitalism - seem to expect Cubans to actually be Che's "new man." Those who point out that it is not so are often seen as "traitors."

Cubans and leader Fidel Castro are practical beings. Che, as minister, was also a practical man. But tens of millions remember him best and honor him most as our idealist, our utopian dreamer, because many of us want to be like him. This is the essence of what Cuba's youth pioneers sing, "Be like Che."

Philosopher Juan Mari Lois wrote an essay on ethics for Prensa Latina in 1995 which I translated. It illustrates what I think about forging communist consciousness.

"Our principal social exaction is the transformation of an alienated human into a free one ... having at its core a system of values that make this person free in their social behavior.

"If we accept the idea that socialism is an ethical option and, above all, an alternative culture, then the educative action of all social agents, including formal education, must be to create and consolidate the formation of a collectivist ethic, an attitude of solidarity which negates and transcends bourgeois individualism. There must also be school programs relating to the ethics of citizenship.

"Our sovereignty, our true independence, also means full liberation, free from old and new forms of alienation, in each Cuban. This collection of freed individualities could then sustain, voluntarily and as aggregated soldiers, the independence and sovereignty that more than one heroic generation supposedly constructed."

Chapter Nineteen: Fidel Leadership

After nearly half-a-century, why is Fidel Castro still the President of the Council of State, in effect, the president and state minister of the Republic of Cuba—the allegedly oldest "dictator" in the world?

As First Vice-President of the Council of State Raul Castro turned 75, on June 3, 2006, the mass media, once again, began speculating on when Fidel Castro would die or be too sick to rule, and if his brother would take over state power.

On June 14, Minister of the Revolutionary Armed Forces (FAR) General Raul Castro held an important speech on the 45th anniversary of the founding of FAR's Western Army, one of three in the nation.

He reiterated that, "human beings are the fundamental component of our defensive power"—part of the "War of all the People", which Vietnamese allies helped establish as Cuba's main defense strategy. Raul spoke of the particular importance of training personnel, both in and out of uniform. There are about 2.5 militia members, one in three adults.

Since the second US war against Iraq began in March 2003, Cuban soldiers, construction workers and volunteers have built hundreds of kilometers of tunnels and fortified many buildings and other works as part of preparation for any military attack from the north.

Raul Castro said that despite the lack of American popular appeal towards US aggressive wars, the imperialists might still attack Cuba, and other lands, as they have often done as, "a way of attempting to get out of an internal crisis."

The Bush regime has even set up a "transitional" government through its new Commission for Assistance to a Free Cuba. It is well financed with several millions of dollars going to internal counter-revolutionaries. The Commission even has a US administrator, who would become a temporary governor of the "freed" Cuba.

Raul Castro concluded his speech by stating that "the founding leader of a Revolution is not transmitted as if it were an inheritance to those who occupy the main leadership posts in the country in the future. The Commander in Chief of the Cuban Revolution is solely and uniquely the Communist Party…"

Among the many articles being written in the months of June and July, one I noted made reference to Oliver Stone's 2004 film, "Looking for Fidel", in which the film instructor asked Fidel the perennial questions about leadership.

Paraphrasing Stone: *Why don't you step down after so many years and let the younger generation take over like Nelson Mandela did?*

Paraphrasing Fidel: The people have the power. I am a spiritual leader. I have been training youth for 50 years. My actual powers are limited. I don't appoint ministers or ambassadors. I have as much power as I do because of my long experience. I am an activist, who puts ideas into practice.

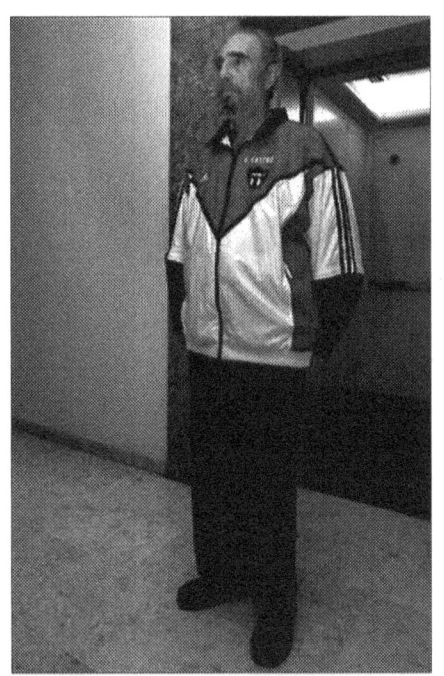

Fidel Castro recuperating in late 2006 from serious intestinal operations.

Fidel explained that his removal is precisely what Cuba's enemies have been seeking since the first year of the revolution. In fact, he said, they have made 734 murder plans against him and scores of them have been put into action.

I am not willing to step down just to please Bush. Why should I help him? I am ready to die with my boots on, working. If you could prove that it would be best for our country, I'd step aside. If I had that impression, I'd step down.

Paraphrasing Stone: *If you died suddenly, it would lead to chaos, it would rock the boat...*

"There are many possible commanders-in-chief," concluded Fidel without naming any.

Who might they be? And how would one come to power?

The Constitution of the Republic of Cuba, adopted in 1976 and amended in 1992 and 2002, provides (Chapter ten, article 94) that the first vice-president assumes the duties of the President of the Council of State, "in cases of [his/her] absence, illness or death."

That would place Raúl Castro in charge until a new election. Raúl also runs much of the Communist party's daily affairs, but the party does not, by law, take part in elections.

The National Assembly of People's Power (parliament) is the legislative organ. Its 601 deputies are elected at electoral districts for five years. There are up to eight candidates in each district.

The parliament elects the highest executive body, the Council of State. Its 31 members then decide on its executive committee, which includes the president, secretary, first vice-president and five vice-presidents. The parliament has unanimously elected Fidel to the Council of State, and the Council has elected Fidel Castro its president since 1976.

The Council of State is responsible to the parliament, which holds two regular annual sessions. Between sessions, the Council runs the government. It proposes laws to the assembly and issues decrees between sessions, all to be approved at the next parliament meeting.

While most pundits of Cuban politics assert that Raúl is the next in line to be president, that would only be the case if the conditions of article 94 existed. Raúl is also one of four possible candidates often discussed, who might be elected as head of state in a normal transition.

Raúl is respected for his good moral conduct. He has a long proven record as a keen manager. He has guided well the defense of the country during nearly half a century, specifically responsible for the nation's defense strategy, and his troops and generals are disciplined and loyal.

Many foreign security experts believe that Raúl might be the best option for stability in the period before normal elections. He would guide the nation with no significant shift in policies. On the other hand, he is old and not universally popular. He lacks Fidel's charisma and diplomatic acumen.

In July, the Communist Party leadership reinstated the party secretariat. It had been eliminated at the beginning of the special period. Many older leaders have been replaced by younger ones. The political bureau, with Fidel and Raul at its head, is revitalizing the party's role.

Other possibilities for a future president include: Vice-President Carlos Lage, Parliament Speaker Ricardo Alarcón, and Foreign Minister Felipe Pérez Roque.

Lage, born in 1951, was educated as a physician of pediatrics. Since early Special Period times, he has been architect of the economic reforms and their implementation, including tourism. The tourism industry produced a two-tiered society, those with international convertible currency and those without, and tempted some junior officials and other employees to engage in corruption.

That left a spoiled mark on the architect, and Raul Castro with FAR took control of tourism. Lage, once thought as a possible successor to Fidel, is probably no longer a realistic option.

Ricardo Alarcón, born in 1937, is one of the most popular, erudite and sagacious leaders. He graduated from the University of Havana with a doctorate in philosophy. Alarcón has had a long diplomatic career since the beginning of the revolution. He represented Cuba in the United Nations and in the foreign ministry, where he was minister before becoming president of the national assembly in 1993. While Alarcón would be an embraceable leader he is thought to be too old.

That leaves the youngest bet, Felipe Pérez Roque. He was born in 1965, and graduated with an electrical engineering degree. Pérez is fiery and quick, and popular too. He took over the ministry post, in 1999, from another young and popular leader, Roberto Robaina.

Robaina was elected foreign minister in 1993. At 37, he was the youngest foreign minister ever.

In 2002, he was expelled from the Communist party for disloyalty, ego-centrism, and for receiving unauthorized money from Mario Villanueva, accused of drug trafficking. Robaina is now working in an urban environmental project in Havana.

Other names can be mentioned, such as the cultural minister, Abel Prieto, but I believe Raúl Castro and Felipe Pérez are the most likely candidates.

In my view, there is no hue and cry, no significant desire or need to replace Fidel. He has nearly full backing by most Cubans for his key decisions and actions. Fidel represents the dignity of the people, but, as many Cubans say, he could not have done anything without their backing.

That belief in Fidel encompasses the general and strong feeling that he *is* Cuba. As the distinguished Uruguayan writer Eduardo Galeano wrote in the "New York Times", May 17, 1992: "Fidel (is) a symbol of national dignity. For Latin Americans, now completing five centuries of humiliation, he is a deeply affecting symbol."

History, as wrote Georgij Plekhanov—Russian Marxist theoretician, who died in 1918—provides, on rare occasions, an exceptional and irreplaceable leader. I maintain that Fidel is one such.

Fidel is also the practical symbol of unity in face of divide-and-conquer Yankee politicians, their corporate owner friends and their military and counter-intelligence forces. And the feeling that Fidel should remain the people's leader expresses a sense not of doom but of fear for what the Yankees might do if he were not there, and an uncertainty about whether the next leader could handle what will come.

For now, and the foreseeable future, Fidel Castro will remain president. No matter who takes over the reins of power after Fidel, there will be a period of national sorrow and of confusion. Most Cubans I ask, what after Fidel, reply: "Ni de pensar"—don't even think about it.

One of my critical thinking friends, Maya, a university professor in English literature, put it this way.

"I admire and respect Fidel tremendously. I don't envy the poor man. Leading this country is the most difficult task in the world today—all these tumultuous world transformations and consequent pressure on us. And, as a people, we are much too hedonistic, garrulous, undisciplined, and too informal to manage rationally. I certainly can't imagine any imbecile from Miami or anyone outside Cuba coming here to 'lead' us.

"Everybody talks about what after Fidel. Raúl is second in line, but he is not popular. Maybe they'd come up with a council of leaders. But I don't see any need for another president today. Fidel is not sick and he is the best."

Then Something Happened

I am neither mystic nor muse, but there is something indescribable about Cuba and about The Horse that simply defies rationality. In those months of June and July, the mass media, crowing the litany of Washington-Pentagon-Langley-Miami, was challenging the Cuban government's very existence. Washington-Pentagon-Langley-Miami's plans for overthrowing the Cuban government had taken an absurd direction. The evil-doers were certain that Cuba's revolution with its socialist sub-structure could not survive after The Man, who was approaching the age of 80. They clamored for his death. And suddenly Maya's desire for the continuation of Fidel as president, and her bid for "what after Fidel", became actuality.

On July 31, just days after I wrote the above description of what the Cuban laws call for if its president can no longer serve, Fidel's personal assistant and member of the Council of State, Carlos Manuel Valenciaga, read on national television a letter Fidel had just written to the Cuban people.

"Due to the enormous efforts made to visit the Argentinean city of Cordoba (and participate in) the MERCOSUR meeting..." followed by visits to the People's Summit, Che Guevara's childhood home, then followed by two speeches on July 26 in commemoration of the 53rd anniversary of the assault on the Moncada and Carlos Manuel de Céspedes barracks...and "with practically no sleep, my health, which has resisted all tests, was subjected to extreme stress and broke down.

"This provoked a severe intestinal crisis with sustained bleeding which obliged me to undergo complicated surgery...The operation obliged me torest for several weeks, away from my responsibilities and tasks.

"Since our country is threatened in such circumstances by the government of the United States, I have made the following decisions:

1. I temporarily delegate my responsibilities as First Secretary of the Central Committee of the Cuban Communist Party to Second Secretary Compañero Raúl Castro Ruz.
2. I temporarily delegate my responsibilities as Commander in Chief of the heroic Revolutionary Armed Forces to...Raúl Castro.
3. I temporarily delegate my responsibilities as President of the Council of State and the Government of the Republic of Cuba to the First Vice President...Raúl Castro Ruz.
4. I temporarily delegate my functions as principal promoter of the National and International Public Health Program to Political Bureau Member and Public Health Minister Compañero José Ramón Balaguer Cabrera.
5. I temporarily delegate my responsibilities as the principal promoter of the National and International Program of Education to Compañero José Ramón Machado Ventura and Esteban Lazo Hernández, members of the Political Bureau.
6. I temporarily delegate my responsibilities as the main promoter of the National Program of the Energy Revolution in Cuba and collaboration with other countries in the area to Compañero Carlos Lage Dávila, Member of the Political Bureau and Secretary of the Executive Committee of the Council of Ministers."

Fidel then delegated the responsibility to the funding of health, education and energy programs to Lage and to Felipe Pérez Roque, minister of foreign relations.

Fidel added that the Communist party "has the mission of assuming the task set forward in this Proclamation."

The Man, whom the US had tried to murder for 47 years, concluded his presidential proclamation with, "I don't have the slightest doubt that our people and our Revolution will struggle until the last drop of blood to defend these and other ideas and measures that are necessary to safeguard our historic process.

"Imperialism will never smash Cuba. The Battle of Ideas will continue forward.

"Long Live the Homeland! Long Live the Revolution! Long Live Socialism!"

There was silence in the nation. Then people poured out their support for their leader as Washington-Pentagon-Langley-Miami ecstatically hoped and demonstrated for his death. But he survived, and on the day of his 80th birthday, August 13, 2006, was seen to stand and walk. The worst was over and he would be well. Almost every Cuban hoped he would be back at his office, hammering away at the Yankees and seeing to it that the plumbing works functioned.

Chapter Twenty: Me and Fidel

January 1-8, 1959. Cuban revolutionaries led by Fidel Castro, Che Guevara and Camilo Cienfuegos take over one city after another. Fidel rides triumphantly into the Mafia city Havana.

I am a frustrated airman in the United States Air Force stationed at a radar base outside Oklahoma City. I hate the military.

When the Soviet Union intervened in Hungary, I was in my last year of high school. I wanted to follow in my father's footsteps and fight the communists. My father had left his factory job to join the Air Force, in order to defend his country after the Japanese fascists bombed Pear Harbor. Following the end of the war, he continued a career as an imperialist soldier.

Fidel and guerrillas in the Sierra Maestra

I last saw him at the US military base in Wiesbaden, Germany where he was stationed in 1968. He "divorced" himself as my father.

The Cuban Revolution had inspired me to join forces against the imperialists and fight for people's right to life everywhere in the world. My first demonstration was on April 19, 1961, in protest of the United States-supported Bay of Pigs invasion.

That day of initial action brought me close to Fidel Castro, the first of four "encounters". He, like Che, is the people's dreamer, and he is also the practitioner, who guides the dream into practice, making it work with its inevitable and mistaken ruffles for eleven million Cubans until this day.

October 12, 1987, Comandante Fidel autographed my first published book, "Yankee Sandinistas". I had met him from afar following a wonderful speech held in Matanzas, Cuba on the 20th year of commemoration of Che's murder in Bolivia, October 9, 1967—an assassination ordered by the CIA, the intelligence service supported by my father.

I had come to Cuba for the first time. It was a leg on my mission to support the FMLN guerrillas in El Salvador. I spent two months in Cuba, and was joyful to learn how much they had accomplished on the road to socialism, relying on sheer guts and a revolutionary morality nurtured by the idealism of Che and Fidel, and so many other leaders and workers, soldiers and security people. Hundreds of attempts to murder Fidel by terrorist forces, military juggernauts and presidents in my homeland had been and are being averted by these dedicated men and women.

The Ministry of Culture invited me to live and work in Cuba, first as a consultant and writer for Editorial José Martí and then as a journalist-translator for Prensa Latina. I lived there in the same conditions as Cubans for eight years. During that time I never spoke with Fidel but did attend press conferences with him present.

As I accumulated experience and knowledge of how the society works, I saw many ruffles and ripples. I was personally bothered by the meetings we workers could attend as part of our work, our block organizations, or, for others, the Communist party and other mass organizations. Most people wanted me to stop talking and asking questions, because they wanted to get home.

I began to learn that most Cubans did not feel that they could make any significant impact on decision-making neither on the job nor in politics. And I was too limited at my own work. I could not write about the true state of the economy or question political policies made at the top. There were taboo areas. I could feel a disappointment setting in.

I wanted to talk to Fidel about this. He was a busy man. He did not answer my request for an interview. There were so many and who was I to take up his time. So, I talked with Fidel in my sleep. I was often angry with him but I always loved and admired him. I found that that is how most Cubans feel about The Commandant, The President, The General Secretary, The Chief of the State Council, The Man, The Horse.

In my sleep with Fidel, I was often entangled in a murderous nightmare. I am in a crowd standing close to where Fidel is speaking. My wary eyes catch an assassination attempt on our leader's life. I cast myself over him and take the bullet. I wake up, but am not sweating as I am when involved in a nightmare over the loss of my own children, who also shunned me for being "anti-American".

This nightmare followed me to Denmark, in 1996, where I still live.

I returned in late 2005 for a three-month reunion with the "last bastion of socialism" and "with" Fidel.

He is as sharp as ever and even more relaxed. Much of what he has fought for is succeeding. And now he has, at least, two other strong, brave and honest Latin American leaders at his side, on the side of the Bolivarian dream of Latin American unity. These seeds can grow into a regional socialist transformation that could assure the independence and growth of Cuba and many other countries.

During my return, I visited many people I had known and met new ones. I did voluntary work at "my" old cooperative farm, watched television news and forums, read many articles and books.

Enrique Oltuski, vice-minister of the Fishing Industry and author of "*Pescando Recuerdos*" (Fishing Memories), explained precisely what it is with Fidel and the people. This is my translation of some of what he wrote about Fidel:

"When the night falls…one feels the throbbing close to the tribunal. One hears agitation, like the sea when it shocks against the rocks; the murmuring of ecstasy, like the sound of the waves against the sand— depending on what Fidel is saying.

"Why does this magical thing occur only when Fidel speaks, when the shadows have fallen and the people can no longer see well but they feel one another? Then sight is unnecessary. It's enough to listen, and feel the people melt with Fidel. Then there is no longer the multitude and the orator, just one people who speak through the voice of one man. Fidel is the voice and the people the body, because, after all, Fidel represents the patria, the native land."

And then the day came!

As a correspondent for the English daily "Morning Star", I was invited to receive the newly elected president of Bolivia, the humble indigenous fighter Evo Morales. A corps of foreign and national reporters stood by the runway alongside hundreds of Bolivian students studying medicine in Cuba. Evo's plane was soon to land. We reporters were tense, not knowing if he would allow us to ask our burning questions.

I had prepared a question for the new hope of Bolivia: How do you intend to confront and win the inevitable conflict between your humanitarian program and that of the profiteering transnational corporations?

What then occurred caught me by surprise. The Man arrived and promptly shook hands with the enthusiastic Bolivian youth. I was standing next to the last Bolivian. Suddenly, Fidel stopped in front of me. His large right hand was slightly extended, still moving in an automatic rhythm.

My hand rose exuberantly to reach his. Then four Rons spoke at once.

Revolutionary Ron: Oh, I want to shake his hand, hug him, to tell him how much he means to me, to us.

Journalist Ron: Now you have to come up with a good question. He is there waiting for you.

Ego Ron: Tell him what your objective is in Cuba. You want to get a book published so that Cubans can read you, so that you can be somebody here in this land of your heart.

Cuban Ron: You must not touch The Comandante's hand. Remember how supposed journalists tried to murder him in Chile in 1971 with a gun hidden inside a TV camera? Fidel's guards will think of you as a potential killer.

The last Ron stopped my hand. Confused Journalist Ron could not think fast enough to dominate the other Rons and asked Fidel the question for Evo.

Fidel, ever the realist, replied: "That is a question for Evo Morales". What a dummy I am, thought I, and the President walked onward.

Later, I told this story to two Cuban journalists. They said that I should have caught his attention by telling him that it was I who had burned my Yankee passport and renounced my citizenship in front of the US Interests Section in Havana, in January 1991, in protest of its war on Iraq.

The following day, I told this story to Antonio Garcia Urquiolla. He was a ship's captain I had sailed with and a double agent infiltrated inside the CIA, whom I had written about in "Backfire: The CIA's Biggest Burn". The CIA had wanted him to assist in murdering Fidel.

His reply to me was: "Ron won the battle of Rons"!

Chapter Twenty-One: Leadership after Fidel

On August 1, 2006, as Washington DC rattled its sabers immediately upon Fidel Castro's hospitalization, Raúl Castro, minister of the armed forces and now the nation's interim commander in chief and interim president of the Council of State, placed defense forces on alert.

On August 17, 2006, Raúl Castro explained why to "Granma":

"We could not rule out the risk of somebody going crazy, or even crazier, within the U.S. government. Consequently...I decided to substantially raise our combative capacity and readiness...including the mobilization of several tens of thousands of reservists and militia members, and the proposal to our principal units of regular troops, including the Special Troops, of missions demanded by the political/military situation that has been created.

"All of the mobilized personnel has completed or is currently completing an important cycle of combat training and cohesion, part of that under campaign conditions."

"It is not my intention to exaggerate the danger. I never have done so. Up until now, the attacks during these days have not gone further than rhetorical ones, except for the substantial increase in subversive anti-Cuba broadcasts over radio and television."

Some of those transmissions were being made illegally from international waters. This violation of International Telecommunications Union rules was not the main concern of Cuba, Raúl explained. It is "above all a matter of sovereignty and of dignity. We would never passively allow the consummation of that aggressive act, and that is why we interfere with it."

This was the second time that Raúl had communicated through the media in the first two weeks of his interim leadership. Every Cuban knew that Raúl was in command at his various posts, and the main one was at "your combat post as always", so wrote the Communist party's daily newspaper reporter Lazaro Barredo Medina.

Revolution Defined

Western bourgeois politicians and their mass media make far too much of Fidel as the only unifying voice in Cuban politics. They have long predicted that with his death, national unity would collapse and "free market" capitalism would take over. I must admit that I came close to believing this too, having heard so many Cubans, including intellectual workers, farm workers, and many party members, say the same when I lived there. Loyal revolutionaries would shrug their shoulders at the question "what after Fidel". Hardly anyone wanted to contemplate the inevitable.

Now that it was happening, the transition of power—or, in reality, the continuation of revolutionary power—was unfolding slowly and people could thus become accustomed to new leadership. Cuba's transition, in contrast to the one planned by the world's terrorist state number one, is not violent or chaotic. This chapter attempts to explain what is happening and why it is happening so orderly.

Raúl Castro concluded the "Granma" interview by congratulating the Cuban people for maintaining faith in their revolution, and thereby demonstrating "confidence in themselves; a demonstration of maturity, serenity, monolithic unity, discipline, revolutionary consciousness and—put this in capital letters—FIRMNESS, which reminded me of the conduct of the Cuban people during the heroic days of the so-called Missile Crisis in October 1962.

"They are the fruits of a Revolution whose concept Fidel summed up in his speech of May 1, 2000...Let nobody doubt, as long as we remain like that, no enemy will be able to defeat us."

"Revolution is a sense of the historic moment; it is changing everything that should be changed; it is complete equality and freedom; it is being treated and treating others like human beings; it is emancipating ourselves through ourselves, and through out own efforts; it is defying powerful dominating forces inside and outside of the social and national sphere; it is defending values that are believed in at the cost of any sacrifice; it is modesty, selflessness, altruism, solidarity and heroism; it is fighting with audacity, intelligence and realism; it is never lying or violating ethical principles; it is the profound conviction that there is no force in the world capable of crushing the strength of truth and ideas.

"Revolution is unity, it is independence, it is fighting for our dreams for justice for Cuba and for the world, which is the foundation of our patriotism, our socialism and our internationalism."

Fidel's definition of revolution includes both ideals and praxis. Not all of these qualities are realized by all Cubans, or even by one person to perfection, but the fact that this is not only the nation's leader's definition of the country's creed but that most Cubans aspire to its fulfillment is the best answer to the internationally asked question, "How can Cuba stand up against the world's mightiest power and do so post-Fidel".

As of this writing (March 2007), Fidel is not dead and may yet return to some of his governmental duties. Nevertheless, his people are now prepared for the inevitable. Seven men have taken over his duties in a "smooth transfer of power". "Unity at home, the message goes, is the best defense against the only external power Cuba still regards as a threat—the United States."

These are not the words of a revolutionary but those of Julia Sweig, an academic spokesperson for the Corporate Global Empire (CGE), which is axisoflogic.com label for the world's hegemonists. Sweig is Nelson and David Rockefeller Senior Fellow—the Rockefeller's are in the center of the CGE—and director of Latin America studies at the Council of Foreign Relations (CFR). The CFR has published the bi-monthly journal "Foreign Affairs" since 1922. Eleven secretaries of state, including mass murderers John Foster Dulles and Henry Kissinger, have been part of its stable.

Sweig's article, "Fidel's Final Victory", in the January-February 2007 issue, is worth citing, because it does what security-intelligence agencies are supposed to do: provide accurate information to CGE's politicians so that they can make "realistic" decisions about how to deal with their enemies, that is, socialists, revolutionaries and, generally, defenders of national sovereignty when this is anathema to CGE economic-political interests.

"None of what Washington and the [Cuban] exiles anticipated has come to pass. Even as Cuba-watchers speculate about how much longer the ailing Fidel will survive, the post-Fidel transition is already well under way. Power has been successfully transferred to a new set of leaders, whose priority is to preserve the system while permitting only very gradual reforms. Cubans have not revolted, and their national identity remains tied to the defense of the homeland against U.S. attacks on its sovereignty."…"Not one violent episode in Cuban streets; no massive exodus of refugees"…"a stunning display of orderliness and seriousness," Sweig observed.

"Despite Fidel's overwhelming personal authority and Raúl's critical institution-building abilities, the government rests on far more than just the charisma, authority, and legend of these two figures…(Cuba) is a functioning country with highly opinionated citizens…Although plagued by worsening corruption, Cuban institutions are staffed by an educated civil service, battle-tested military officers, a capable diplomatic corps, and a skilled work force. Cuban citizens are highly literate, cosmopolitan, endlessly entrepreneurial, and by global standards quite healthy."

Raúl Castro and the six others, Sweig continued, "have been running the country under Fidel's watch for decades,"..."preparing for this transition to collective leadership for years"... "Fortunately for them, Fidel has taught them well: they are working to consolidate the new government, deliver on bread-and-butter issues, devise a model of reform with Cuban characteristics, sustain Cuba's position in Latin America and internationally, and manage the predictable policies of the United States. That these achievements will endure past Fidel's death is one final victory for the ultimate Latin American survivor."

Frothing in blind hate, Miami politicians have become all the more desperate given the reality, which Sweig describes as the enduring legacy of Fidel. These ruthless men and women of power still fear The Horse as he slowly recuperates. Congresswoman Ileana Ros-Lehtinen, a close Bush ally and the Republicans Foreign Relations leader in the House, publicly called for Fidel's assassination even as he lay on his sick bed. This was corroborated by the pro-terrorist Miami daily, "El Nuevo Herald", on December 24, 2006.

Collective Leadership

After half-a-year of collective leadership, the seven temporary replacements for Fidel's multi-duties are fulfilling them assiduously, albeit not at the tireless pace of their leader.

Raúl, for example, reserves most of his evenings for his family. He spends most of his work day out of public view. Only occasionally does he greet visiting dignitaries and review military parades. His daughter, Mariela Castro, who heads the National Center for Sex Education, told a BBC reporter, in September 2006, that her father is not at all like the Western mass media paints him.

"He is warm, a romantic lover and passionate for my mother."

Vilma Espin, president of the Federation of Cuban Women and often a roving ambassador for the nation, is Raúl´s long-time wife. Mariela has both parents' blessings in her drive to end all discrimination against "sexual deviants", that is, homosexuals and transvestites.

Those close to Raúl do not see him as a stiff person, rather glad and witty in private. Unlike his five-year older brother, Raúl likes to dance. They both share an appetite for the world's best rum produced by their kinsmen. Everyone respects Raúl's discipline and reliability when it comes to defending the nation. He is a man of the army, a man of the party, and not self-sufficient; he emphasizes the collective. The Western mass media, submerged in individualism, cannot describe him accurately exactly because he is not self-proclaiming.

And although this same media portrays Raúl as a hard-line military man, he is a spokesperson for opening up the media and other public platforms for greater critique from the people. In September 2006, he told congressional delegates to the nation's unions, CTC, that union officials must be with the workers at their job sites, listening to their complaints and input.

"As has been said many times...one of the most difficult challenges in ideological work is to achieve that the worker feels that he is a collective owner of the wealth of the society and acts accordingly." "...It is most difficult to achieve in the daily work."

Raúl went on to indicate that the lack of this feeling contributes to

Fidel and Raoul Castro

corruption and thievery, to other illegalities and to a lack of work discipline. Therefore, it is all the more imperative that workers' are listened to and that their ideas are incorporated in work site, local and national economic planning.

Raúl Castro, implies Sweig, is just the person to succeed Fidel, because there is "a widespread sense that Raúl is the right man to confront corruption and bring accountable governance, [which gives] the current leadership more legitimacy than it could possibly derive from repression alone..."

And "the regime's continued defiance of the United States" also helps.

With this frank statement, Sweig is admitting that almost all Cubans and most Latin Americans, including many mainstream political parties and national leaders, see the moral and economic value in "defying" what CGE contends is the world's greatest democracy and land of freedom.

Even a key leader of United States' war machine, Defense Intelligence Agency Director Lt. General Michael D. Maples, told AP writer Anita Snow, on January 19, 2007, that Raúl is firmly in control and "will likely maintain power and stability after Fidel Castro dies, at least for the short-term."

The second man most mentioned in the leadership collective is Carlos Lage. As a volunteer doctor, he served on a medical mission in Ethiopia. Lage has been the main architect running the controversial pro-market economic reforms since the start of the "special period".

Like Raúl, Lage is also a vice-president. As such, he has represented Cuba at many international gatherings. Lage administers many governmental affairs and is Fidel's replacement to overseeing the energy program, from saving electricity domestically to cooperation with oil-suppliers Venezuela and other countries, a task that he is successfully fulfilling.

Many political observers, Cubans and not, believe that after Raúl, either Lage or Pérez stand the best chances for being chosen future president of the Council of State and president of the government.

The minister of foreign affairs, Felipe Pérez Roque, 41, is the youngest of leaders. Before becoming minister, he was Fidel's chief of staff, and is said to be one of the closest persons to Fidel. Pérez is part of a team of three—along with Lage and Francisco Soberon, director of the Central Bank—in charge of funding the three key international programs: education, health and energy. Although Pérez has not been much in the limelight, he played a major role in at the international summit of non-aligned nations, in September 2006.

In a December 5, 2006 speech, Pérez stressed the role that ethics and moral values play for the Cuban revolution, and for Fidel personally. "Ethics is the reason of the State", he said. The ends do NOT justify the means. Pérez pointed out that torture and assassination are never permitted, and that there is no evidence that such occurs. Pérez spoke of how Fidel holds talks to military, state security and prison personnel about this. Cuba's ethics include aiding poor people in many "Third World" countries without any profit motive.

José Ramón Machado Ventura, 76, heads the Central Committee's organization department and is now responsible as well for co-supervising

Cuba's international education program. Since taking over his new duty, he has represented Cuba in various arenas, including at the inauguration of Nicaraguan President Daniel Ortega, January 2007.

José Ramón Balaguer, 74, is the new minister of health. He was the party's ideological chief and considered a hard-liner. He, like Machado, fought alongside Fidel and Raúl against the Batista regime. Administering and promoting international health aid programs is his new task and there is no visible sign that these efforts have declined.

In fact, a USamerican writer, Karen Lee Wald, who lived in Cuba many years, interviewed Mariela Castro, December 2006, about the sex education center's work and how it was being received by state leadership. Mariela recounted that Balaguer is "wonderful" to work with.

The center is proposing to the Ministry of Public Health that it approve transsexual operations and that these people should be able to register their new sexual identity. Mariela said that center personnel gave Balaguer a book about this and he asked only when they were going to begin.

Esteban Lazo, 62, is an economist. He took over the party's ideology department from Balaguer and is in charge of the educational programs along with Machado. Lazo held many posts as party head in different cities and provinces. He is considered to be one of the party's most powerful men and the most visible black leader. Lazo headed Cuba's delegation to the U.N. General Assembly in September 2006.

All seven leaders are national assembly delegates and members of the Communist party central committee. All but Francisco Soberon and Felipe Pérez Roque are also members of the party's leading political bureau.

These seven will probably continue running these programs, and government and party affairs, even if Fidel begins to take on some duties again. He will do so, I believe, in an advisory capacity. The next election, in which members of the Council of State will be decided, is scheduled for the spring 2008 during the provincial and national assembly. If Fidel is alive, it will be a matter both of his health and of the best policy for leadership transition that will determine whether Fidel will run for election again.

2006 Economic Advances

According to Sweig, another reason why the transition of power is working so well is because the government continues a viable "entitlement program", delivering goods and services.

At the end of 2006, the National Assembly, under the chairmanship of another of Cuba's leading figures, Ricardo Alarcon, delineated the progress and challenges of these multiple socio-economic programs. At 12.5%, economic growth was never greater. The previous year, with Fidel at the reigns, the 11.8% growth rate was also unprecedented. The medium growth in Latin America was less than half that, at 5.3%.

The main reasons for such dramatic growth was increased production in national oil and gas, lucrative oil agreements with Venezuela, greater sales of nickel to China, increased tourist revenues, and a 90% augmentation in the export of biotechnological products to 50 countries.

In the area of health, infant mortality fell from 5.6 to 5.3 per 1000 births. Despite economic hardships, infant mortality has fallen by 43.6% since 1995. Havana has but 4.9% infant mortality and the largest is in Santiago de Cuba, at 7.9%. New born babies have a greater chance of survival in Cuba than in the United States, where the infant mortality rate actually rose slightly to 7.1%.

Delivering the good and services, especially energy growth with electric savings, has advanced under the direction of Lage. Eighty percent of Cubans had received modern kitchen appliances by the end of 2006. Most everyone had received one or more of the 29 million electro-domestic utensils/apparatuses handed out or sold at cost. There are several more electric plants and almost no black outs. Electric production grew by 7.2% with less electric wastes.

Every family now has energy saving fluorescent light bulbs and new fixtures: 9.5 million were passed out free of charge. One in four families received new, energy saving refrigerators.

Natural gas is now in use as a by-product of the nation's crude oil. With four million tons, Cuba now produces nearly half their energy use, five times what it did in 1989. In addition, there is great advance in the use of natural energy, wind and sun especially. Seven thousand solar energy generators have been installed in many schools and health centers.

The key challenges are in supplying adequate housing and public transportation. But even here, the advances over the previous year and earlier ones are impressive. At the outset of 2006, the government promised to construct 100,000 new residences. Such promises have come and gone many times without being kept, yet 110,000 new residences were, in fact, built, which was three times 2005 results. Three times as many buses were added to the network over 2005, from 135 to 550, including 300 school buses.

Cuba's leaders are increasingly acknowledging that the government and party had made errors in placing too many restrictions on "intellectual liberty". Minister of Culture Abel Prieto told the writers association, January 2007, that during the 1970s, hard-liners conducted "witch hunting", especially against homosexual intellectuals. Many of them have been apologized to and several persons once censored are now in leading positions. Some, such as Antón Arrufat and Miguel Barnet, have been awarded the national prize for literature. And, as I have indicated in Chapter 15, the media is much more open to critique than ever before.

Conclusion

What after Fidel? An apt response to this age-old question is the twist which Mertxe Alizpurua captured when interviewing Iroel Sánchez, president of Cuba's book institute. (See rebellion.org, January 6, 2007).

"The correct question ought to be what will happen to the world, in Latin America, after Fidel. In Cuba, there is a revolution, and in Latin America as well. The answer to what will happen after Fidel is in Venezuela, Bolivia, Ecuador and in Nicaragua."

In her own way, Sweig seems to agree.

"Latin Americans, still deeply nationalistic, have long viewed Fidel as a force for social justice and a necessary check on U.S. influence." "Despite Washington's assiduous efforts, Cuba is far from isolated; it has diplomatic relations with more than 160 countries, students from nearly 100 studying in its schools, and its doctors stationed in 69."

When Fidel dies—and it might be many years yet—the nation will mourn. But the nation will not fall apart. People will have had many years, I believe, to get used to the idea of a collective leadership, which ensures greater checks and balances and greater difficulties for bureaucrats who wish to be corrupt.

It was ingenious of Fidel to place six men in charge of the supervision and financing of three great socio-economic programs. And no one fears that Raúl will become corrupt in his old age, after 48 years of military and party leadership. In fact, as I wrote earlier, with his leadership in the ever-vulnerable-to-corruption tourist industry, he wiped out some corruption, including most of the visible prostitution.

Growth statistics reported above show that the new leaders are on mark. Moreover, Cubans are proud of their world status. As a writer colleague, Celia Hart, wrote (see rebellion.org, January 19, 2007) in her intimate essay, "Fidel desde mi balcón" (Fidel from my balcony):

"...we are summoned to defend the socialist revolution of the world... This is, perhaps, the only consolation left me when I learn that the graceful shadowy profile of Fidel vanishes forever, leaving white and empty the borders of my useless balcony."

Chapter Twenty-Two: Beyond the Crossroads

I concluded my 2006 "Morning Star" series with this title, because I called my 1994 series, "Cuba at the crossroads". I was worried that what socialism there was would evolve, at best, into a social welfare state.

The leadership was also worried about the derailing of socialism. With the fall of European state socialism, the island was all the more isolated, and the people, as a whole, were passive. Corruption and thievery were rampant.

Fidel and Raul Castro held one speech after another against these internal negative characteristics. In Raul's 1994 speech, "Si, se puede" (Yes, one can), he signaled "the start of a campaign against passivity, routine and bureaucracy."

Today, progress is undeniable. Besides the many economic and social advances already delineated, I cite a few concluding positive indications—Cuba has moved beyond the crossroads.

In contrast to a plethora of prostitutes and hustlers, these opportunists are now rare. I never frequent tourist spots where some prostitutes are said to hang out, but there are fewer and they are not walking the streets. Some young men still hustle stolen cigars but they are fewer and they are more wary of being caught.

Thanks, in fact, to the fall of Comecon countries, many Cubans are more self-reliant and more responsible workers. Thanks again, in fact, to the tightening US blockade, there is greater patriotic consciousness. Cubans, as a whole, may not be as revolutionary as many supporters believe but they are determined to defend their sovereignty against foreign invasion.

While "no coges lucha" (don't fight city hall) is still a common motto, some Cubans are acting to overcome that anti-revolutionary attitude. There are initiatives in some "barrios" (localities) by social workers and participatory sociologists to stimulate people to involve themselves in projects to improve the community.

A friend of mine, Maritza Lopéz, is one. She was the organizer and director of the young cultural-dance group known as Haralaya. Once it dissolved, she joined others in the "Paulo Freire" community house, in Havana's La Lisa district.

They teach people to think critically, to get involved, to pressure the local government to meet basic needs often neglected, such as garbage collection and the repair and painting of residences. They seek to shape natural leaders from the "barrios".

The Martin Luther King Center, in Marianao, Havana, works similarly, in addition to promoting brotherhood across borders, in King's spirit.

Often, though, when engaged with old or new acquaintances in the perennial discussion—how goes Cuba—they point only to the negatives, even calamities.

One such calamity is the poor judgment—in my opinion and for some Cubans—made by top leaders in trusting the enemy, something rarely done by Cuba's leaders.

In 1998, Cuba was still reeling from a series of bombings at tourist hotels. One tourist had been murdered. Cuban leaders hoped the FBI would do something to stop this, but it was a security and foreign policy mistake to believe that the FBI would actually assist Cuba by stopping their Miami friends' terrorism against Cuba. It was over-optimistic of state leaders to give the FBI documentation of Miami terrorist activities and plans for more terrorism.

Instead, the FBI figured that much of Cuba's information must have come from their sources infiltrated into the Miami terrorist groups. This led the FBI to find out who they might be, and that ended in the arrest of the Miami Five.

I bring this up to point out that this mistake cost five good men many years in prison, which could discourage other brave patriotic Cubans from deciding to infiltrate the enemy in the future.

I make this case also to point out that the best of leaders make mistakes of judgment and actions, and thus there must be some mechanism to prevent as much of this as possible, or when mistakes are made that there must be mechanisms to criticize and change them, in order to avoid as many as possible in the future. Some call this "checks and balances". I mean that there is all too little of this in Cuba.

Che Guevara often spoke about this need. In a 1961 interview with Maurice Zeitlin, Che stated:

"Our task is to enlarge democracy within the revolution as much as possible…We feel that the government's chief function is to assure channels for the expression of popular will."

In Che's famous ideological essay, "Man and Socialism in Cuba", published in Uruguay, in 1965, he noted that: "The institutionalization of the revolution has still not been achieved. We are seeking something new that will allow a perfect identification between the government and the community as a whole."

Back to Raul's 1994 speech. If the working class was really opposed to "passivity, routine and bureaucracy" why did it not initiate its own campaign against them?

This is so, first and foremost, because the working class does not control the means of production or the country's internal and external politics—not directly. Union leadership has some input at top levels, but union leadership is appointed by the top.

There are no demonstrations without the top authorizing and organizing them. Strikes are not permitted, although they are technically not illegal. Communist party directors do not allow real grass roots debate about policies in the media. Critique only occurs when leadership decides to take up a controversial theme.

I do not propose opening the media or demonstrative platforms to pecuniary tributes, but I do suggest that the media be opened to true probing voices of Cuban workers. A debating society can be dynamic, healthy.

The main hindrance to worker control, to real socialism, is the world domination by capitalism and imperialism. The fact that the United States lays but 150 kilometers away is the greatest hindrance.

I believe, however, that if the Cuban leadership had had more trust in the working class back in the mid-60s, once US military attacks were turned back and the internal counter-revolution defeated, the leaders would have gradually turned over to the working class significant say in productive relations and in making local and national politics.

Nevertheless, I must admit that I am uncertain that this would ultimately have been in the best interests of the working class or for Cuba's existence. One can not know if, in fact, most workers were capable or interested in taking a socialist-communist direction. Cuba's leaders could not have known if the working class would have sustained that fight long enough to win it had there been true democratic decision-making. Perhaps, they knew what was best for the workers.

No one likes to hear this. But, as Lenin told us, we must face facts as they are and history as it has unfolded. A true democracy has never been tried. No working class has had the power or exercised the power to build socialism or any system. Perhaps, as some interpret Marx, it can not happen until world capitalism is defeated and swept aside so that the construction of socialism by the working class itself can begin.

So what does that mean to us Cuban solidarity activists, to us leftists? It means that we continue our solidarity work, continue fighting against the evil system of profiteering-individualism, and continue educating for a collective system run by and for us all.

The only difference is that we drop the illusion that a few million people living on an island just off the Yankee coast can, in fact, create socialism all alone.

Socialism must be forged regionally, at least. There must be equal trade partners. There must be more democracy in day-to-day policies and in production, or the workers will be passive, thus less effective, wasteful, careless and corrupt. That is to say, alienation of labor will be extant, as it is.

The state and Communist party—both essentially guided by one irreplaceable man—still control the society. Yet more authority and decision-making has been decentralized since a decade ago. Decision-making, however, is still made by a few leaders. The working class, as such, still awaits decisions from above, albeit some of that is now localized.

French writer Danielle Bleitrach noted, in her May 18, 2006 article, that Cuba's "participatory democracy" excludes spontaneity. "Without a doubt, the exterior pressure and threats, very real, are limiters; it is a democracy of war. But there is debate." She concluded that, "probably there will have to be a far more public debate, much more `ideological´, when a series of problems have been solved..."

Regardless of whether Cuba has achieved socialism—it is a process, after all—the Cuban people and the government are more than worthy of our love and support. They have done no harm to the world and they have helped many millions of people.

They have held out against "the enemy of humanity" to quote the Sandinista anthem. In so doing, they have held out hope for billions of us.

As filmmaker Humberto Solás said, let us not expect Cuba to be the salve of our consciousness. For the joyous people they are, for the inspiration they are to us, we owe them our energies. If Cuba falls, we would all be the poorer.

Footnotes

1. See Fred Royce's "Cuba Today: Agricultural Production Cooperatives and the Future of Cuban Agriculture" for a more thorough study of contemporary farming in Cuba, within an historical persprctive (email: froyce@ufl.edu).
2. See Philip Agee's "Inside the Company: CIA Diary", and my "Backfire: the CIA's Biggest Burn".
3. Many of these essays and articles have been translated into English by CubaNews: its editor, Walter Lippman, has collected Celia Hart's selected writings in a book titled "It's Never Too Late to Love or Rebel" (Socialist Resistance, London: 2006).
4. A Cuban merchant ship attacked in international waters with machine gun fire and streams of high-pressured water on January 30-31, 1990, by the US Coastguard vessel *Chiconteague*. This poem is dedicated to its crew who sailed onward to their Mexican harbour destiny with bullet holes in their hull and other damage.
5. *Palmiche* is the Spanish word for Royal Palm berries.
6. *Palmitos* is the Spanish word for palm straw.
7. *Yagua* is the Cuban-Spanish word for Royal Palm bark.
8. *Mambi* was the resistance name for those Cubans who fought Spanish colonialism and later the US's neo-imperialism. *Campesino* is the Spanish word for small farmers.

Cuba: Tenaz Palma Real

Avenidas de Palmas Reales que se mecen en la brisa
alineándose esplendorosamente erguidas
altas y orgullosas.
Immortalizada en la canción Guantanamera:
"Yo soy un hombre sincero de donde crece la palma"
con su ondulante tronco y oscilantes hojas
danzando como la bella Guantanamera.
La Palma Real fielmente arraigada en el fértil suelo como sus hijos nativos
firme como la resistente tripulación del barco Hermann
impávida ante el fragor de los hostiles truenos.
La Palma Real hogar sagrado del poderoso Changó
emperador del mundo, el más temido y deseado de los dioses;
palmitos y hojas en lo alto hacen que su trono
arroje llamas sobre sus enemigos que se estremecen ante su fragor
mientras su noble Palma Real defiende la soberanía en el escudo nacional.
Changó dios del fuego del relámpago y del truenos
come aves y cerdos cebados con el palmiche de la Palma Real
cura enfermos con sus raíces
hace que sus mujeres barran el polvo con su florescencia
envuelve los tabacos con la yagua
construye casas con sus tablas y techos con sus palmitos y hojas.
Majestuosa Palma Real
lugar de cita del guerrero de ébano
su esbelta Ochún de cobre
elegante trío el de ellos:
Changó aterrador devorador de fuego, ardiente amante
Ochún diosa de los ríos
deidad de sensualidad y amor
Palma Real galería para aventuras divinas
sombrilla que desafía las lluvias y los rayos hostiles
amparadora de las tierras de cultivo
albergue del aborigen, del mambí, del campesino
refugio del tocororo
que luce los colores soberanos de Cuba
pájaro nacional rebelde
que prefiere morir antes de ser enjaulado.

(Dedicado a la tripulación del barco Hermann)
Por Ron Ridenour, La Habana, diciembre de 1991
(traducido con Coralia García)

Cuba: Tenacious Royal Palm

Avenues of Royal Palms sway in the breeze
splendrously erect they straighten
proud and tall
undulating trunk and pendulous fronds
dancing like the Guantanamera belle
immortalized in her song:
"Yo soy un hombre sincero de donde crece la palma".
("I am a sincere man from where the palm grows").
Royal palm faithfully rooted in fertile soil like its native sons
resolute as the implacable crew of the freighter Hermann[4]
unflinching before hostile thunder
whilst their noble Royal Palm
shields the sovereignty in the national coat of arms.
Chango god of fire, lightning and thunder
        dines on chickens and pigs fattened on the palmiche berries[5]
cures illness with palm roots
has his women sweep dirt with its florescence
        wraps cigars with its yagua bark[6]
        builds house sidings and roofs with its palmitos and fronds[7].
Majestic Royal Palm
rendezvous for the ebony warrior
his svelte copper Ochún
elegant trio they:
Chango awesome fire-eater, ardent lover
Ochún goddess of rivers, deity of sensual love
Royal Palm gallery for godly escapades
umbrella rod before hostile rains and lightning
protector of farm lands
        shelter for aborigine, mambi, campesino[8]
refuge for the tocororo
wearing Cuba's sovereign colors, this obstinate national bird
who chooses to die rather than be caged.

Also available from Socialist Resistance:

It's never too late to love or rebel

"It's never too late to love or rebel" is the only book by Celia Hart to be available in English. Walter Lippmann, the editor of CubaNews, has selected and edited the documents in the book.

His collection contains Celia's best-known articles written since 2003. It contains a number of recent articles including an interview with International Viewpoint.

It has an attractive full-colour cover and is printed professionally in the Demy octavo format which is most widely used by modern publishers. It is available online, from Socialist Resistance and to booksellers through Ingram's global book distribution network.

To order your copy post-free, please send a cheque or international money order for £8, made payable to Resistance, and send to us at PO Box 1009, London N4 2UU, Britain.

www.ingramcontent.com/pod-product-compliance
Lightning Source LLC
Chambersburg PA
CBHW031255290426
44109CB00012B/597